AF435272

Cycling Through the 70s

The Transcontinental Trip that Inspired a Lifetime of Bicycling

By Lynn Natal Hartman

Photographs by Paul Hartman

ISBN 979-8-224-91978-9
First Edition May 9, 2024
https://www.lynn-natal-hartman.com/
Flagstaff, Arizona

To my favorite photographer and my best friend.

Thanks for keeping my tires pumped all these years.

Table of Contents

1 HORIZONS | California 1

   2 We Were Young Then | 2024 Reflections 39

   3 COAST| California . Oregon 49

   4 Earth Day | 2024 Reflections 81

   5 RIVERS | Oregon . Idaho . Wyoming 91

   6 MOUNTAINS | Idaho . Wyoming 129

   7 Meeting Challenges | 2024 Reflections 161

   8 PLAINS | Wyoming . South Dakota 167

   9 Looking Back ~ Moving Forward | 2024 Reflections 199

   10 MIDWEST to EAST COAST 205

Afterword 237

Paul's Journal #3 239

Acknowledgements 245

Transcontinental Bicycle Tour
4,311 Miles

*

106 Days

*

10 States

*

13 Flat Tires

1  HORIZONS

California

The road stretches out beneath the overpass all the way to the horizon. There's a spot in the distance where two lanes appear to converge and meet at a single point. In art, this illusion is called the *vanishing point*. If you are a curious sort, the view does not stop there—curiosity leads to temptation. Paul describes it best, the tugging at the imagination and sense of adventure. It makes him want to go exploring, out beyond the place where the road becomes a tiny dot. Every time I watch him gazing off toward that fantasy point in the distance I recognize the same sensation in myself, and I'm resolved to be beside him, wherever the horizon takes us—together.

Journal Entry ~ June 9, 1974 Our first day out, we're camped in my parents' backyard. Roosters crowing in the neighbor's yard woke me up. We'll be leaving so many things behind this morning—roses blooming in my dad's garden, fruit ripening on his apricot and orange trees, that family inside, still sleeping, who will be following our progress on the map hanging on their dining room wall. We'll leave behind familiar lifestyles, long-developed routines and relationships that have been building our foundation. Just around that corner, at the end of the street we've known for so long, we face new challenges, learning experiences, and wild dreams. Just extensions of the life we've been living, but today there's no limit to the possibilities. Nothing to stop us in this moment, we will follow the eternal yellow morning sun as it moves across the sky and carries us forward into our new life.

Morning came, we were leaving, and we were pumped. It was like we were the first ones ever to try crossing the country on bicycles. Everything we owned was packed away at Bekins Storage, except the 35 pounds packed onto each bike. We'd said goodbye to the rented house, the job, our friends. The family was next, but I didn't want emotional goodbyes to spoil our start. Everyone gathered out on the drive to get hugs and wish us well. But we kept the fears submerged, confirmed our plans to keep in touch with them once a week by pay phone, and pushed off.

My two younger brothers followed us to the edge of town in the old red GMC pickup, grabbing shots with a super-8 movie camera. We stopped on the last overpass to take some still photos and they waved us off on our adventure. We headed west along California's Highway 1 from Santa Barbara till the coastline turned north. Once we were beyond the city limits, rolling through open land along the ocean, we knew we were really on our way.

Paul looked over at me. "Do the legs feel okay?"

"Sure. Not bad riding on the freeway, is it?" I shouted back. *This is going to be fun*, I thought. What a perfect day for a beginning. Sun had burned off the morning fog, there was only a slight breeze, and the bicycles were tuned up and riding smooth.

That day was full of firsts, which we were quick to point out to each other. For our first lunch stop at Gaviota State Park we rested under the shade of sycamore and oak trees. We celebrated with a toast of pink lemonade (from a powdered mix). Soon after, we came to our first significant hill.

"How long is this going to go up, anyway?" Paul wondered aloud. Our leg muscles were strong enough to take the hill, but our road bikes only had 10 gears: 5 in back and 2 large rings in front. He was always better at using the low gears to gain advantage on the uphill stretches, dropping into second or even first gear to make the pedaling easier. I had not yet grasped the idea that gears are there to ease the workload. I was rapidly running out of breath as I tried to power through in 5th gear, straining my thigh muscles to the max.

"I think I may want to walk to the East Coast!"

Reaching the crest of that hill was a triumph, and we slowed to savor the feeling of accomplishment as we took it easy, resting our legs on the downhill side. We were definitely eager to keep riding. We rode until about 6 p.m., with plans to stop for the night in the small coastal town of Lompoc. We'd had a good start and were in for a good night's sleep at the end of 54 miles. Coasting to the bottom of another long, sloping hill, we rounded a corner and suddenly the countryside was behind us and we were steering down the main street of town.

"We're here! What are we going to do next?"

We rode slowly down the deserted street, looking right and left, hoping for some sign: PAUL AND LYNN, YOU CAN SLEEP HERE. Someone had apparently forgotten to put the sign up—no one knew we were coming.

Paul had an idea. "Hey, let's just ask someone."

"There seems to be no one around to ask. There's City Hall and the Police Department. Do you see any police?"

And just then a city patrol car drove past us. We tried to flag him down, and finally he stopped at a traffic light. We caught up and waved him over to the curb where we stood straddling the bikes. No smile, not a word, he just sat there watching suspiciously from inside the car and waited for this petite twenty-something girl wearing cutoff jeans and braided hair to finish rattling off her story.

"Hi, we are on a trip on our bikes and want to camp out tonight. Do you know of any places around here like campgrounds or anything? Somewhere we can rent? Someone's yard, or any place where it's legal?"

"Nope," he said. He only knew of one state park, 20 miles out of town. But that was south, and we were headed north.

I moaned at the thought of more miles. "Isn't there anywhere? Do you have any ideas, just a place to pitch a tent? What about a city park?"

"Where are you two headed, anyway?" He pulled off his shades and seemed to me to be getting a bit friendlier; maybe we were simply feeling more relaxed.

"Well, this is the first day of our trip. We're going to the East Coast."

"Really?" he smiled. He directed us to a tiny trailer park that allowed camping. Checking in with local officials or law enforcement actually turned out to be a good strategy whenever we found ourselves tired and hungry in a small town with no idea where to stay. Often the town parks offered the best shelter for us and we appreciated the hospitality. This guy was the first of many small-town officials who helped along our way.

At the trailer park we found there was space for us so we registered with the quiet gentleman in the office who wasn't too impressed with our mode of travel. We found a vacant spot against a concrete wall to pitch our tent. I heated a can of Dinty Moore beef stew for dinner in the laundry room, out of the wind, and we fell into our sleeping bags just as the first chilly blanket of beach fog rolled in.

I fell asleep wrapped in the joyful knowledge that all my dreams were coming true. Newly married and tucked into a tiny blue tent with the man I loved, I drifted into sleep thinking about all the choices we'd made to be here. In the short few months of this magical romance we were building our future together.

The Plan. The story began two months after we were married. Paul and I were totally goofing on the idea that we were at the very start of our new life together and wondering at the possibilities.

Although the political scene in 1974 was exploding with the Watergate scandal and Nixon about to be impeached, the vibe in the Santa Barbara beach town was bright. Paul and I didn't have a car, so one day we biked to the newly opened Ecology Center where I was fascinated by the variety of back-to-nature goods available in this interesting new shop. It had only been a few years since the devastating oil spill from offshore drilling in the channel. After protests and marches against "big oil" wiping out the beaches and wildlife, the locals had created this store and celebrated the very first Earth Day in April, 1970, to show the peoples' respect for Mother Earth. We browsed aloe plants, handmade leather headbands, and vegetable seeds for the garden.

Then we cruised Hazard's Cyclery, the local bike shop where we found a flyer about plans for a group bicycle ride across the United States. In 1976, bicyclists all over the country would celebrate America's 200th birthday with "BikeCentennial '76," a trail route being mapped from coast to coast. They were looking for people to test different routes. We stopped for ice cream at McConnell's and couldn't help talking about how we might make a trip like that. Through the window I could see the two bikes leaning on the palm tree—mine green, his white—the shiny spokes sparkling and winking at me.

On the way home, we checked out the local bookstore and found that Rand McNally had just put out a large sized, state-by-state road atlas with all the main highway routes. We were flipping through the maps, wondering where the bike route would be going, when a friend saw us and stopped to talk.

"Hey, Lynn! What's happenin' ? Planning a trip?"

"Mmmmmm, yeah..." I answered quietly. This was just a spark of an idea, and I wasn't sure whether to openly express our secret desires just yet.

"Oh? Where to?"

"Well, we're just imagining taking off on our bicycles someplace. Maybe across the country..."

It was a nice topic of discussion as I was getting to know what life with Paul might be like. We spent a couple of evenings examining maps in the atlas, wondering which road looked like what. And then the book was set on the shelf next to our small collection of vinyl LPs, favorite novels including my favorites by John Steinbeck, Paul's "Hitchhiker's Guide to the Galaxy," and a couple of college textbooks.

We went about our daily lives, planted the garden, started refinishing an old dinghy to sail in the harbor over the summer. From the beginning, I tried to make our back-to-nature lifestyle reflect our mutual respect for Mother Earth. All the while I was working eight hours a day, Paul was picking up odd jobs and we started putting half our earnings into a savings account for someday when we figured out what we wanted to do with our lives.

After supper a couple of weeks later the traveling idea came up again. Paul was gazing out the window, watching the horizon; he could see the ocean and clear blue sky from our house on the hillside. I couldn't believe the direction the conversation took as we washed dishes.

"I can't stop thinking about that bicycle trip across the country. What would it be like if we went this summer?" he asked.

"I don't know," I thought for a minute. "I bet you and I could actually do a ride like that."

"Not with the group planning the route for 1976. I mean just you and me. Now! Want to just do it?"

I looked up at him and tingled with the same electric spark that first drew me in when we met four years ago.

"Well, we've always known we're supposed to be together. Maybe this is the reason. Do you want to?"

"Is there any reason to wait any longer?"

"None, I guess. Wouldn't that be a trip? To blaze the trail on our bikes, to ride all the way to the Atlantic. I could write, you could photograph; we would be explorers!"

That night, and for a few days afterward, we found ourselves constantly thinking about it. This was a compelling idea, and since we were itching for adventure, the idea finally took hold. A week went by and we had not changed our minds.

My first entry in the journal I would keep for the entire trip:

Journal Entry ~ April 22, 1974 We're going to get on our bikes with sleeping bags and rain gear and chart the country with camera and pen. And keep moving as slow as we can until we've seen all there is to see—from the West to the East side of this continent. We're floating in a bubble of excitement, half expecting it to burst if we laugh too hard. Paul thought we should give the idea some time to mature—to think, and pray, and listen, and not decide till a week has passed. So we did. And then we made our decision!

I gave my notice at the utility company where I worked the switchboard. Paul gave up a few choice gardening and landscape jobs. A week after that, two sets of panniers came in the mail. We had them trial-packed in the first five minutes—the first of several times. And then we knew we were going. I'd always held a sense of wanderlust. To be on the bicycle, I'd have the opportunity to connect with the land and people in ways not possible by any other means of travel.

The Road Atlas became our main source of reading. Poring over states and interstates and noting the elevation marks at the mountains—we were looking at the Rockies.

"How do you ever think we'll pedal over the huge passes? I don't see how we can make it."

In our hearts, neither of us could imagine we *wouldn't* make it, so we decided we could at least try. Nothing seemed impossible. We were optimistic that this bike ride would not be that difficult to manage. Together we would work out what to bring, where to start, and just ride, camp, and figure it out as we went along. Each morning in the month of May we woke up to a map of the Western United States taped to the closet door.

The next few Saturdays we traveled many miles shopping from one end of town to the other on our bikes (even then we didn't have a car). Limited space made it easy to decide what would be necessary for survival. We packed only what we had room for and ended up eventually sending some of that back. We sought advice from books, other bikers, and bike shops. I even contacted the editor who ran the bicycle column in the local newspaper, just to tell him about our plans.

The 12-inch difference in our heights did enter into the planning. We couldn't even ride each other's 10-speeds. Paul's frame was 25″ with the seat post raised another foot, to accommodate his 6'3″ frame. I chose mine especially for shortness. I rode a 21″ men's bike, me standing at 5'2″. The size of the tent was a little bit of a problem. We picked out an open-ended tube tent, just long enough for Paul to stretch to either end. But then later as we sewed in the velcroed mosquito netting it got a little touchy. I don't think he ever did sleep straight, but most of the time we were too exhausted to worry about it. There were advantages to taking along a 6-footer on a trip like this. Paul could describe to you his 101 ways to pitch a tube tent in 106 distinct locations. Most of the good ones included attaching the ropes to a branch or roof top entirely out of my reach—sometimes even out of my sight. But I never had to worry myself about where I'd sleep. Figuring out the gear was easy because, as it turned out, we only needed one another.

ONE WAY

One section of the main street in Santa Barbara on the way between our house and my folks' house included a flat, straight stretch with wide enough shoulder for the two of us to ride side by side and talk. Every time we pedaled that strip, and then simultaneously leaned into the curve and glided into their street, Paul and I could feel deep inside what it was really going to be like to pedal our way across thousands of miles of country, side by side, with just the wind and the sound of the wheels surrounding us.

The Route. Our route was determined by approaching summer weather. We would ride north to avoid hot deserts as much as we could. Paul's parents were living just above New York City, along the Hudson River. That would be our destination, making it a coast-to-coast trip when we included my relatives in Rhode Island. Starting at the Pacific Ocean in Santa Barbara at my parents' house, we aimed to end our trip with a stop at Paul's parents' place. Then, we'd continue on to dip our toes (and wheels) in the Atlantic. Adding stops at a few interesting landmarks would break up the tedium of riding provided a great spirit-booster.

We left with the intention of restocking in San Francisco after 300 miles to see what we'd done wrong or forgotten. Nothing had changed once we hit San Francisco, except the budget. But that will come up later on in the story. We somehow lost a sack full of carefully chosen tools in Oregon. We made it the rest of the way with a screwdriver and a wrench.

What We Brought. After working out how we would camp over the summer in a variety of places, all our equipment needed to somehow fit on two bikes. Bungee cords worked to wrap our two down sleeping bags, pads, and the small tube tent that rolled into a stuff sack and all of that hooked onto the rear racks. We cooked on a mini propane stove and used a set of nesting pots made for backpacking. Our small first aid kit included only a few items we put together ourselves. An extra 32-oz water bottle plus our bike mounted 16-oz bottles would give us a day's drinking water. The plan was we'd shop every couple of days and divide up the food between our packs. Two packages of freeze-dried meals provided some emergency rations.

I carried a front bag full of junk. I had my notebooks and pens, small camera, toothbrush, hairbrush, bandana, and quick snacks. Paul had his front bag full of camera equipment and film. We also carried a small Frisbee. We brought a minimal amount of basic bike tools, a tire repair kit, spare brake pads, and tubes.

We kept our clothing choices very light: a pair of cutoff shorts and jeans each, two t-shirts each, a couple of crop tops, a long-sleeved shirt and light jacket for me and denim long sleeved shirt for Paul. We brought three changes of socks and underwear each and wore sneakers. Wool sweaters, hats, and gloves kept us warm when evenings got chilly, and we found waterproof hooded rain parkas that wadded up small and were useful windbreakers. We budgeted ahead of time for quality film: the best quality, the best processing and enough of it so Paul would be free to shoot anything and everything that came into his focus on this once-in-a-lifetime trip. We didn't want to miss any great pictures. Carrying our limited amount of money in paper traveler's checks helped so we would spend our savings carefully.

Paul's advice for someone planning would be not to consider weight as much as cubic inches of items to take along. So many times we repacked and rearranged a whole picnic table's worth of stuff into a couple of one-foot-square packs. It got to be tedious after awhile just trying to find room every time we stopped to camp and then repack all the pieces each morning. We were envious once, when we watched a long-haired fellow coast by us smiling away on a 3-speed rusted bike with a plastic bag strung over his shoulder holding only a jacket and a cotton sleeping bag! And most bikers we met agreed unanimously that it would be such a fine trip if we could have all done it on naked bicycles. One more thing we kept in mind: traveling by bicycle would be a sound environmental choice. Earth Day and the oil spills had left a bitter taste for traveling by automobile and using gas.

Food Shopping. We needed to carefully consider our eating routine—food would fuel our trip. With limited space, on a pre-determined budget, we couldn't imagine how we would carry enough snacks on board to satisfy our cravings. I had a tendency toward vegetarian eating and Paul hated vegetables; I cooked Italian style at home, and he liked Chef-Boy-Ar-Dee canned spaghetti. We found out campsites would cost a couple dollars per night, which meant our daily food budget would be limited. So there was a lot of compromising. Not compromising with each other, but with our hunger and the foods that would be available on the way.

First trip to the market to pick up supplies:

> "Too bad we can't take eggs, but they'll spoil, and break, and
> be awful. How about cereal?"

"How about granola instead, more nutritious...? And milk...powdered milk. Huh?"
"I hate powdered milk."
"That's the only choice we've got."
"Well, I'll eat dry granola." Mine usually ended up in plain water.
"Can we get a salami?"
"What for?"
"For lunch, and snacks and stuff."
"And carrots. We need carrots."
"Carrots are terrible."

"You like them, remember?"

"Okay, I'm getting one salami anyway."

And we wanted quick energy food. We figured we could mix our version of gorp: m&m's, nuts, jellybeans, hard candy, and raisins. We weighed the bags of candy at the fruit counter—four pounds—more than our entire cook kit and stove weighed. The candy was colorful, but it lasted about two days, then we dumped it. We tried Bisquick, and learned how to make flat biscuits fried in butter that came in a squirt bottle. This became a staple: it filled us up easily, cheaply, and it tasted like fresh baked bread after a day's ride. Dried soups and fruit made up our lunches, and we experimented widely with dinner menus—spam and beans, beans and bread, bread and noodles, cheese and noodles, noodles and spam, and sometimes tuna. We were always starving, so it was always delicious.

California Camping Day. A few days after our start I developed a deep appreciation for basic needs essential for our survival: food, water, shelter, all these things we used to take for granted.

A day would go by, riding along the California coast:

"Can you believe we're really here? Just look at the rocky beaches below."

"So blue! The wind and waves make me feel so wild and free."

"Sounds like the heartbeat of the ocean, right down below us."

"Can you believe the crazy wind?"

"I can hardly get going downhill against this headwind! I'm never, ever riding this coast again, in this direction!"

It was beautiful, and it was hard, all day long. Then we'd pull into camp.

"Hey, it's free. No $2 charge here. This is great." Our original daily budget had not included campsite fees, so whenever we could save that cost, we were thrilled.

"Okay, pick out a good tree."

"The ground has to be level, no rocks or lumps." Paul wanted everything to be horizontal, so all the blood wouldn't rush to our heads or our feet and keep us awake.

"Here's a good spot."

"No, it's too far from the bathroom (outhouse)." That was my main concern in the middle of a dark night.

"Aren't there any spots with tables? We want someplace to eat."

"Okay then, we can use this tree and string the tent rope across to that low branch. But you'll have to squeeze to get in."

Road weary and hungry, I tried to organize the meal.

"Where's the water faucet? I didn't see one, did you?"

"Can you hand me the pots please?"

"This table is slanted. The stove won't sit still."

Then I'd ask, "Do you want the spam in slices or chunks this time?"

"Sure smells good, can we eat yet?" was Paul's refrain as soon as the food hit the hot frying pan.

Nothing was ever well-done, water never boiled more than 20 seconds after the first sign of bubbles. Supper was divided into exactly half, and we ate in silence. It usually took 15 or 20 minutes for the entire preparation-to-eating process start to finish. I'd clean the pots whenever water was available (it was in abundance on the coast and near rivers, not so easy to come by as we got to drier climates).

There were a few odds and ends to putter over before darkness fell. Paul made notes on the map and we talked over plans for the next day's ride. Our journey was plotted region by region or state by state on small, detailed maps we picked up when we could. This allowed for flexibility on our route by giving us a more intimate sense of distance, terrain, towns, and points of interest we could incorporate on the way. My faithful daily journaling also usually happened after dinner as I tried to make notes of all we had seen and done. It wasn't long before sleepiness would creep up on us. When the natural light disappeared, we happily halted our day's activities.

"Are the sleeping bags spread out?"

"Yeah, let's go use them!"

"Lock up the bikes, and cover those dishes, okay?"

Inside the tent, for a minute or two:

"It's nice being here, isn't it?"

"Those people we talked to were so friendly."

"Remember that fun hill today..."

"Okay, I really need to go to sleep. Good night."

Blankets of unconsciousness surrounded the tent for 10 hours, sometimes more.

Then, the sun popped out, the world awakened, and nature jostled us from sleep. Mornings were chilly, and there'd be another gnawing in our stomachs. So we were up, eating breakfast, and on the move quickly to keep warm. We adopted a very regular routine—we felt good, strong, and close to nature, because we were living in rhythm with our surroundings, no artificial comforts to cushion or distract from the basics.

We were doing a huge amount of physical activity, enjoying immense mental stimulation, and we were forced to find the resources in our own packs to carry on each day. There was simply nothing more to think about except what we'd find around each bend in the road. We were very preoccupied by everything there was to see and do and never paid much attention to our legs circling around and around, the wheels spinning out the black road beneath us. It was only the first week, but the biking seemed to be automatic, pleasant, and we were adapting to our new way of life.

Hill Work. A closer look would reveal the truth: each small hill, further and further into the day, loomed mountainous out in front of us. We fought gravity and headwinds, hauling our bikes loaded with gear up a steep incline with only our leg muscles pushing us. It was tough, tiring, took my breath away. But I was ready for this work, and actual pain wasn't usually an issue. At the top, as the hill leveled out, I was fully recovered and ready to tackle another. Neither of us ever had to walk up any of the hills. Most of those hills rewarded us with a freewheeling downhill coast on the other side. It amazed me that none of the discomfort or discouragement lingered once I gained the top.

I had my own way of tackling a hill, which made Paul yell at me more than once; feigning anger, but more frustration, because if the hill were no more than a slight rise, and no longer than two miles or so, I usually beat him to the top. By then I had figured out the gear ratios, so I just threw the bike into lowest gear, raced to the summit as if in a run, and got it over with before I had a chance to get tired of pedaling uphill.

"Where do you think you're going? You can't go that fast up this hill. You'll wear yourself out."

"It's the only way I can do it, sorry."

"There's no reason to race like that, I can't keep up with you. And I wouldn't make you go faster than *you* wanted."

We were both panting by this time, Paul maybe a few feet behind me and losing ground. Then, as was often the case, there was a sharp steep few feet right at the top; he'd come up alongside me and slowly, steadily move right on past; I was wiped out and had used all my energy racing to get to the top—Tortoise and the Hare style! We made it up all the hills that way, and that's really all that counts, not technique. I also began to appreciate more about being with Paul, that I could be myself while always having his support.

It never occurred to us that we'd get tired of riding the bikes and we never did. During the awful headwinds along the coast we were disheartened and we wanted to be riding the other way. But it was mostly comfortable to be just riding the bikes down the road, day after day, mile after mile. We were the vehicles that provided the opportunity to see, smell, feel, and experience so many special things around us, and we knew no other way of travel save walking that would allow us such intimate closeness with the land.

Journal Entry ~ June 10, 1974 One and a half hours since breakfast at Lompoc. What a thrill, riding a 3-mile downhill coast on our second day. I caught the sweet, moist smell from a swampy lagoon nestled in the green and yellow and white flowering hills. Wildflowers lined our path all morning and the photographer has been busy at work. I'm watching Paul, balancing his bike just off the roadway, camera out, to capture the colors. I am taking advantage of the moment to pull out my journal. The only sounds in this valley are birds and ducks and insects—and I'm smiling cause the sun just peeked through the fog. I've never before written on location but, straddled over the bike, pen in hand, nature is my pure inspiration.

Meeting People. We were heading toward Santa Maria on the freeway when we discovered a peaceful road outside Vandenberg Air Force Base would make for more comfortable biking. A tedious series of small hills and then a long downhill coast brought us to a strip of empty lots, some run-down homes and buildings, mostly deserted, stretching across a little valley. We weren't even sure at first if it was really a town.

We decided to stop and check it out. Paul was taking pictures of the front of the Casmalia post office when a woman came out and inadvertently got into the photo. Her demeanor and the flowered house dress she wore reminded me of my grandmother. I waved and walked across the road with my bike to speak to her as she stood in front of what seemed to be the only store in this lonely town. It was boarded up and apparently had been closed for a while.

"Hi, good morning! I hope you don't mind that my husband just took your picture while he was getting a shot of the post office. It's a good way to record the names of towns we ride through," I said.

"Oh, my! No of course I don't mind. It looks as though you are heading somewhere far. Where are you traveling from?" she asked.

"We left Santa Barbara yesterday morning, and just rode here from Lompoc."

She smiled and looked over at Paul. "That sounds like quite a journey. And where will you two be going from here?"

"Well, our goal is to ride to New York. But we're just starting out..."

"That is certainly an ambitious plan. I am very interested to hear more about this. My name is Mary Granden, and I am happy to welcome you to our little town. Would you like to come over to my house and visit for a bit? The coffee's made and I'm sure my husband would also like to meet you." Her smile was warm and welcoming, so we walked with her down the road and around the corner to her modest home.

Inside was cozy but it took a moment for my eyes to adjust to the darkened room. Unaccustomed to being inside after days of riding and camping, I wondered why there was no sunlight until I noticed the old-fashioned crocheted lace curtains covering the windows. Her living room was overrun with books and knickknacks on every surface, a piano at one end and a fireplace at the other.

Paul and I sat close on the overstuffed couch and chatted with her husband while she fixed a tray of coffee and yummy homemade cookies for us. When she joined us I told her a little bit about how we chose to get on our bicycles and explore the country while we had the chance, before we settled down.

"Oh, yes," she said, "I think it's just wonderful to see you young people taking the opportunity to see what's out there and find out a little more about the world. I have been staying in touch with pen-pals from different countries for many years. It's impressive that you can ride your bikes on a trip like this."

She told us she had been in Casmalia most of her life and raised four children there. All four studied through the 8th grade in the old one-room schoolhouse. The school district had just completed a new two-room school with a multipurpose room. Mrs. Granden explained she and some of the other townspeople had started meeting at the school to find ways to keep the whole place from having to relocate and incorporate into a bigger town. The locals had hopes of someone reopening the store, and maybe a little bar on the corner. They were worried about a new toxic waste disposal facility that just opened in the hills above the residential area the year before.

Toxic Waste. It was heartbreaking to hear about their concerns for what might happen and we sympathized with her. I was alarmed to hear about the dump and the effects it was already having on this small town, but that day it was difficult for me to wrap my head around why businesses and government representatives would allow something really toxic to harm people living nearby. We finished the snacks and were a little anxious to be on our way. At the end of our visit she and her husband held our hands and said a short prayer to wish us a safe journey. We promised to stop by again if we're ever in the neighborhood.

Soon I realized that our appearance provided a great ice-breaker. Wearing tattered sweaty clothing, looking lost, or asking directions, always at the peak of adventure, we tended to attract people to open up and talk to us. This was a new and invaluable experience, to find with just a few easy smiles and words I could turn the attention away from us and learn so much more about such a variety of people. We were meeting and getting to know interesting individuals in their environment, places, and circumstances we knew nothing about. We met so many fun, warm, and helpful people at every town and even out on the road. The more we talked to people we met, we found they each had a story we would learn from. We also discovered much about the unpleasant facts surfacing in the early days of the environmental movement. Casmalia was our first exposure to this growing concern

Journal Entry ~ June 11, 1974 The ride from Guadalupe to our tent at Pismo Beach was tense and harder traveling than we'd have liked. It took us through rolling farms and then a mesa thick with the scent of eucalyptus groves. It was a narrow two-lane road with sandy shoulder and heavily traveled by large trucks. We are getting to appreciate flat roads more and more. Bodies are a little burned and chafed. My skin is probably the first place I've suffered. Stiffness comes in the morning crawling out of the sleeping bags and then in the afternoon getting off the bikes when we walk to stretch our legs a bit. In between, the riding is mostly comfortable and gets more exciting with every mile. I'm sleepy now. We saw the sun just before it set tonight.

Pismo Campground. We ticked off familiar beach towns as we rode past Pismo, Avila Beach, San Luis Obispo, and Morro Bay. Our approach from the south led us beyond Point Conception, marking the place where waves crash into shore directly from the west. I noticed how the sea changed from the calmer, south-facing beaches of Santa Barbara. Foaming breakers were huge, over my head sometimes 10 feet high at the crest, and water whipped up the sand on the rock-strewn shore. Since we were familiar with this part of the coast, we chose the smaller paved paths that took us closest to the ocean wherever we could escape the busier Highway 1. Most mornings in early summer started in damp fog, and later in the day the sun burst out and sparkled across the surface of the sea. A swampy scent of reeds growing in the creeks filled the gray mist with a sensation of living things, comfort, and warmth.

My body was getting harder, muscles stronger and more rigid, ready to meet the power and flex of the steel bike frame under me. That silent sound of the road bike cruising fast on smooth surfaces put me in perfect sync with the flow and physicality of the ride—riding along in sync with Paul—our shared goals coming true. We stopped briefly at the gated dirt track leading out to Piedras Blancas Lighthouse Station. Just three days in the saddle and we're cruising into the expanse of mellow green valleys at a river mouth and the beginnings of the mountain range that forms Big Sur headlands.

Big Sur Magic. Big Sur exists because of the coastline's unique and complex topography and geology. A great diversity of rock—granite, sedimentary, and metamorphic—creates a dramatic and highly volatile 90-mile stretch of land. The Santa Lucia Mountains were molded and formed on top of active underground faults along the Pacific plate. Land along the sea edge is continually being carved and eroded as seasonal storms form over densely forested hills and valleys. Creeks fill and overflow, carrying earth, vegetation, and debris through curved narrow canyons to the sea. Landslides reshape and wear away the craggy edges of rocky cliffs. These steep cliffs are buffeted by white crashing breakers at the edge of the redwood forest. It is the greatest meeting of land and sea on the continent.

The southern edge of this rocky shoreline appears just past grassy pastureland near William R. Hearst's Castle, built in 1947. We stopped the bikes at the funky Sebastian Store in San Simeon. Monterey pines spread their wind-blown branches toward the shore. It was at this old wood cabin store that we stumbled upon what would become a favorite habit—sharing a quart of cold milk and downing a box of sugary Hostess-O's raspberry-filled donuts. From that day on, whenever we happened on a gas station or convenience store mid-morning, we would stop and fill up for a sweet treat—often right on the side of the road, sitting on pavement.

In the early morning there was no one around, only a fog bank falling down the hillside and across the meadows. Through a magical mist I could make out dark bluffs and the start of the winding wonders of Big Sur. Along this undeveloped stretch of coastline, only accessible by Highway 1, also called Cabrillo Highway, the sea sounded almost musical. My body vibrated with high notes and low notes navigating each hairpin turn along the Big Sur Highway. Close in where the low waterways flow to the ocean, then high up the bluffs the road twists around sharp curves overlooking the water, the ride felt rhythmic and paced.

Electric Vibe Ride. It's not that I could actually feel the electricity in the air, but I sensed a new kind of vibration, nevertheless. Excitement encompassed and energized my ride from Big Sur onward. The air along the north-central coast is indeed infused with negatively charged ions that are created whenever water churns and crashes against the rocky shoreline. Headlands, cliffs, and huge boulder outcroppings are scattered from eons of storms as tides pull and push the tides and the surf into the beaches and cliffs. Windblown and wild, all the power of the sea carried me forward and released mood boosting endorphins, sweeping me into the natural high that comes with bicycling along the Pacific. I would never forget the sensation. Me and the sea—connected for days and days of excellent riding.

Journal Entry ~ June 12, 1974 We're stopped at Ragged Point and the beginning of the spectacular views in Big Sur. As we rode out to the forested point on a rough dirt trail, we passed dozens of monarch butterflies dipping into wildflower nectar for breakfast. They are migrating and finding shady protected spots among the soft-needled Monterey Pines and cypresses to rest in their travels along the coast. Black and gold wings drift up into the blue sky, waving to the waves below. Every wild bush is in full flower, bursting out of the rock walls and smiling at the day—wild sages, lupine in purple and yellow, and waving mustard grass. I think back to when Paul brought me here 3 years ago, my first experience seeing the spectacular beauty of this place, when we were getting to know each other on that first summer camp out. I knew then that I'd be back, with him. It feels right, getting to know the intimacies of Big Sur inside us, moving at our own pace, under our own power. Together, at one with the universe. This is where it's at.

Soon enough, the daydreaming and musical ocean sounds were interrupted and brought into sharp reality. We were fighting strong headwinds from the north, navigating a crazy narrow shoulder of road beside motorists in speeding cars, many towing trailers and motor homes. I was trying to take in the incredible scenery going by as hill after hill after hill made progress slow and frustrating—uphill to the bluff, downhill into the creek bed, uphill again, downhill once more. I kept gaining, and then losing elevation, forced to ride back up the next hill after having just ridden down to the bottom. There was a fine line between the agony of the wind and mountainous climbing and the ecstasy of headlong coasting down the hillsides toward the blue sea. I gripped the handlebars hard and kept the straps on my toeclips pulled tight for maximum power as the incredible scenery kept me pushing forward. At the end of a fighting and frustrating yet beautiful day, we had only covered 40 miles.

Salmon Creek. We stopped early and had a quiet afternoon walk among the trees. The forest service camp along the Big Sur River, nestled among redwoods and sunshine, sat just a bend in the road away from the ocean. We made a cozy camp under lush pine boughs after our first glorious day in Big Sur. We set up just close enough on a hillside where we could still hear the surf crashing on the rocky shore. I had been away long enough from the din of cities and parking lots and the sight of billboards to realize that I really enjoyed this lifestyle. Living outside agreed with me, and Paul was using up enough film along the coast that I worried he'd run over budget.

The peaceful surroundings provided still more of a change from riding into headwinds, and I quickly recovered from the discouragement I had about the hills. We took off early the next morning, enjoying the blue sky and blue sea instead of the continuous coastal fog we had been riding in. There was a clear advantage to getting an early start, a few miles gained before the traffic and trucks were out. Then fog rolled in and soon turned to rain. I rode through some showers with a tailwind. Even though I was getting wet, I welcomed the boost from the wind.

Summer rains continued in between sunshine and breaks in the clouds. I was surprised to discover riding in rain is quite comfortable while wearing shorts and it was easier than trying to ride in water-soaked jeans. The hooded parka held my body heat in and kept me mostly dry. It wasn't cold in June in California, and we learned to take advantage of laundromat dryers along the way.

Other Bikes. At the top of a high hill in Monterey we were just setting up camp in a small park.

"Paul, I think there are some other bike tourers over there. Let's go say hi."

We were both still a bit shy around strangers at this point, but we felt something in common. When we found out how far they had ridden we were a bit intimidated. We were, after all the miles we'd covered, still in the early stages of our ride.

Paul ventured over. "Hello, where are you from? We're on bikes, too, over in the next camp."

"We just rode from Chicago!" The accents gave them away, a girl and a guy about our ages, looking like they were on top of the world, strong and lean and grinning ear to ear.

"Wow, really? We're headed that way. To New York, or maybe Cape Cod. What was it like riding that far? Did you just get here to the coast?" He couldn't stop asking questions.

They set up camp and had supper, then walked over to our picnic table. We talked for awhile, comparing notes. We wanted to hear about the highlights of their trip, and why they decided to do it. As it turned out, the girl was a state cycling champion and had some touring experience as well. She had just left a laboratory research position to take this bike trip. Her companion told us the worst part of the whole ride was—no surprise—wind blowing against them the whole way. They described the vast expanse of flat lands with nothing to look at and nothing to mark their progress. They had spent most nights in motels, but near the end of the ride had run out of money so they were forced to camp out every night.

Their fastest, longest day was 130 miles, riding into Denver and excited for that milestone. They were covering 80 or 90 miles in an average day. Together they expressed their most heartfelt wish, that they could do the whole thing again back to Chicago but taking all their equipment off the bikes and riding with the wind behind them all the way back. It had taken them 52 days to cover half of what we planned to do.

It was really a boost to my morale, to meet some people who had actually done it. They were not the last we would meet brave enough to ride a long distance on bicycles. Some individuals we met even did it alone. Each bicyclist we encountered became a special someone to us—easy to talk with, great to share stories with. We felt a strong bond because we could empathize with shared experiences. No one but other bike riders knew exactly what it's like pushing the pedals uphill into a headwind. We were all pioneers, making our way under our own power on two wheels in a land overtaken by cars and trucks and mass transport.

Monterey Bike Path. Outside Monterey we found one of the nicest bike paths of the whole trip, and I thoroughly enjoyed the smooth, quiet ride through eucalyptus groves and rolling sand dunes. The path went on for 10 miles alongside the highway and railroad tracks. It was paved and wide and allowed for a beautiful ride with no hassles from traffic or narrow shoulder. We were beyond the serenity of Big Sur and all that wild, natural wonder. After the lovely ride through Monterey as we headed toward Santa Cruz, I had even more reason to miss the quiet of forest and park lands. The weather was uncomfortably wet, and there were no campgrounds except a commercial camp set up for trailers, with no spaces designated for bike camping. The charge was $5 a night, even for bicyclists. We had to choose from rows of rectangular, hard-packed dirt sites between cars and trailer campers. It did not seem fair to me, and we spent a very miserable night—too close to flashlights, generators, and radios.

Turning a little more inland for part of the next day's ride, we found ourselves in farm country once again, reminding me of Lompoc. Among rolling hills and flat farmlands, I noted farm workers and trucks laden with fruit and vegetable harvests, drivers who were not on the lookout for bikes on the roadway. This area of Northern California made me think of Steinbeck country, the Salinas Valley just inland from Monterey, where stories of migrant workers from the depression era were not so different from today's migrant farmers following the seasons to earn their living. We were constantly moving as well, observing vivid slices of life as we traveled.

A little two-building settlement called Davenport had a tire pump where we stopped for a break and met a family—mom and dad and two young sons bicycling the coast route south to Los Angeles. We exchanged camping information, and they warned us of rain ahead. The rain caught us, and we got pretty wet right away. That night we stayed in a little rustic motel just off the highway because of the weather. Paul was fighting off a little cold, and the stormy weather moving north threatened to drench us if we camped out overnight. Not enough sleep in the noisy KOA the night before convinced us it would be best to get a good night's rest where we could stay warm and dry.

What's that Sound? The morning dawned clear and sunny; the two-lane road took us down a long curving hillside through a stand of pine trees; tree trunks growing close together darkened the forested path. A metal barrier left a narrow shoulder along the steep road and I took off riding well behind Paul, coasting through the trees.

Off in the midst of the forest I thought I heard chain saws, but I cruised along enjoying the sensation of floating, smelling the fresh evergreen scent, and watching blue patches of sky winking between the shadows. After about two miles, the road opened to four lanes and I was surprised when suddenly a double-trailer semi-truck passed me, way too close! The sound I'd heard was not chain saws, but the truck's air brakes blaring on and off—the driver had been unable to pass me all the way downhill and had to slow to my speed on a downhill run. I was pretty shaken at the thought of having held him up all the way from the top. Paul was waiting for me at the stoplight at the bottom, he had seen the truck fly by and couldn't believe I'd been oblivious to the giant vehicle on my tail. Embarrassed, I begged for a donut stop as soon as we could.

It was our ninth day out, and we knew we were within a day's ride to "The City"—San Francisco. I could feel the expectation swelling inside, realizing we'd just ridden 300 miles. The legs couldn't go fast enough. The wind in my face was incessant, I wasn't even noticing the trees, hills, and flowers. On the way out of Pacifica, the southern outskirts of San Francisco, signs posted on the road ahead of us read: "Pedestrians, Bicycles, Motor-Driven Cycles Prohibited" on the only road heading north. This was the first road restriction to hinder our progress.

"Oh, NOooo! Bummer! Now what do we do?" I exclaimed.

"Want to hitchhike?" Paul ventured. "They can't do this to us after we've pedaled all this way, and against all that wind! I'll ride illegally—there's no other way!"

On the corner of a small cross street we just sat down. I was stunned, faced with the first multilane freeway of the trip. We just waited. It was the way Paul and I often handled problems we encountered on our journey—sit still and listen—we had faith things would work out somehow. Luckily for us, problems always seemed to turn out okay. At that moment, we were determined to ride into San Francisco before the day was over.

"Hey! Look across the street!" I shouted. Just opposite us on the side road—two, three, four, no—six bicyclists came around the corner from the other direction, all with packs on, and looking like they had come from a good distance north, exactly where we were headed. They turned onto the other side of the divided highway and cruised away down the same road we had just come up.

"Hey, Hey! Hello. Is that the way to San Francisco?" I was waving and yelling. But Paul had already mounted up and was crossing the street, so I followed. He took the road they had come out of, which led us through some housing tracts. Eventually it wound around and across the freeway on an overpass and continued all the way to San Francisco. Elation carried me along the side streets as we came closer and closer. I was pointing hysterically at everything I saw. We made our way through more neighborhoods. Paul navigated us through and around the traffic; we were nearing the familiar outskirts of the City by the Bay.

2 We Were Young Then

2024 Reflections

Celebrating my shiny new e-bike in 2024, it is nearly the 50th anniversary of our transcontinental ride. This year I've completed over 1,000 miles of riding, my worn out knees wrapped in fuzzy leg warmers and the joints in my hands protected with long-finger gloves against the winter chill.

I can't believe we made that trip fifty years ago. In my heart, it does not feel like any time has passed. There are so many differences when I prepare for a ride these days: battery charge, check; electrolytes in the water bottle, check; special bike shoes for pedaling dirt paths, check; helmet; gloves; cell phone with Bluetooth and GPS location apps open. Back then, it was simple to keep warm, when our young bodies generated enough heat just being alive. Comparing today's ride with the day we hopped on our two-wheeled ten speeds and took off on a 4,300-mile trek across the continent, it seems everything's changed.

Yet, many things are exactly the same: The thrill of the ride, just me and the bike and the road beneath me. Riding is freedom. Riding is restorative. Riding is energy. I gain strength, and health, and I get to see and experience the day, the view, breathing fresh air deep into my lungs, energizing every part of me. It clears my head and lifts me up. Paul and I encourage each other every day to get out and ride.

A Magical Meeting. I treasure the idea that we still have shared goals, similar interests, and the same desire for discovery. The magic of our relationship shines brightest when we are in a new space, seeing something for the first time, uncovering a surprise and catching its light together. The horizon still tempts us.

We met one afternoon in 1970—I got in the way of Paul's camera while he was shooting an architectural assignment, a church steeple up the street from where I lived. When I saw this good-looking guy standing out in the field grinning at me, waiting for me to get out of the scene, I was embarrassed, but he seemed friendly enough—tall and thin, hair the color of sand just long enough to brush his shirt collar. I waded through the tall grassy weeds and apologized for ruining his picture, but he smiled and said he didn't mind. That smile crinkled around his green eyes—same color as mine. He showed me his 4x5 camera mounted on a tripod and let me stick my head under the black cloth to look through the viewfinder. I had to stand on tiptoes to see. Amazingly, the image was upside down, and he tried to explain what that was all about. After we chatted awhile I told him I had to go home, pointing out my house on the corner. I headed back down the hill. In a few minutes I was surprised to see he had followed me home and was knocking on the door. He met my parents, briefly. Then he asked me out to lunch.

Adventure Dates. Going out with Paul was never a traditional dinner-and-a-movie date. He'd pick me up in his 1965 VW Notchback (an oddly shaped sedan he called The Red Baron). I'd be wearing a miniskirt, my hair done up, and maybe sandals with a little heel, thinking we'd go to a restaurant. Every single time, we ended up grabbing something to go from a fast-food place or a market and walking barefoot on the beach. He'd carry my shoes. After sunset, we'd go down to the harbor to watch the lighthouse blinking out on the sandbar. On weekends, he'd take me for a drive to explore someplace that we'd never been before—along the coast to see some waves; off the beaten path on a dirt road to see what we'd find; up the pass to catch a view of the ocean—the horizon stretching south and west from the hills above Santa Barbara. There were enchanting journeys of discovery where we'd end up in a place like Big Sur or the Grand Canyon, we were always finding something bigger than ourselves.

Paul charmed me with his photography, his imagination, and his adventuresome spirit. I was twenty years old, I felt I had lived through a lot, and yet I understood very little of the world. The lens through which I viewed life was focused then by my elders and authorities—parents, educators, newspapers, and television. Their views did not explain the parts of the world I was trying to make sense of. What I saw through their lenses was blurry, out of focus, and did not answer my questions. It seemed like turning binoculars around and seeing everything shrunken and miniscule. I wanted a broader, clearer view. Paul had a different way of seeing everything, a view that enchanted me, and I wanted to see more of what he had to show me. Our excursions were simply a precursor to our eventual bicycle ride across the United States, to discover the world together.

Doing Our Own Thing. It makes sense to me now, thinking back to the turmoil swirling throughout the nation as I came of age, how I had the impulse to take off on my bicycle. The social, cultural, and political circumstances in the 1970s were unique. We were unique. Both Paul and I were of the generation that rejected the establishment, questioned authority, and imagined a way to make the world better. It was our imperative to be independent and rebellious in the face of the events we were experiencing.

The Vietnam War was raging, the U.S. involvement began in 1961 and by 1968-1969 the country was fully engaged in the war. I remember listening to body counts on the nightly news, a frightening and constant reminder of what my generation was facing. I thought of boys I knew, school friends, my own brothers whose birth dates, thankfully, saved them from the military draft determined by lottery. Paul joined the Navy to avoid being drafted into the Army.

The fight for civil rights, voting rights, women's rights was exploding, spurring more protests and riots. Five influential political figures were assassinated over six years: Medgar Evers, 1963; John F. Kennedy, 1963; Malcom X, 1965; Martin Luther King, Jr., 1968; Robert F. Kennedy, 1968.

College campuses and communities across the country were in constant upheaval, and that was a key reason I did not go away to a four-year university in 1968-69 after I finished junior college. The country wasn't going in the right direction. I was disillusioned. How would I focus on studies while grappling with student protests and civil unrest? In 1970, Ohio National Guardsmen opened fire on demonstrators at Kent State University and four students died protesting President Nixon's unauthorized escalation of troops. The authorities I had been raised to respect were murdering and injuring kids my age. I just wanted out.

I started seeing Paul after he had served four years on a ship off the coast of Vietnam. While he helped launch and land planes that supported troops on the ground, I was watching news events unfold on TV. My part in the sit-ins and marches was minimal: a couple of junior college hallway demonstrations; standing on the sidelines of protest marches on the main street in downtown Santa Barbara.

By the time of the 1972 Watergate scandal and Nixon's impeachment was looming, none of us could really make sense of any of it. Folk singers and hippie poets of the times became leaders of the new culture—Peter Paul & Mary, Bob Dylan, Joan Baez, Neal Young, Aretha Franklin—their songs were the anthems we all could relate to. Music triggers memories. Listening now to the old songs brings me right back to those confusing times, and I hear the voices of youth crying out for a better world. We broke free from the traditional choices of our parents' lifestyles. We were ready to make our own way.

Equipment Differences. We didn't have much in the way of convenience when we rode out that day on our adventure. Road bikes were stripped down to the basics. Ten-speed was the standard for the steel frame bikes: 5-gear cluster on the back and two rings in front. Shifters were awkwardly located on the downtube. The bike I had was a metallic green Raleigh International, and Paul rode a white Batavus.

Brake pads were hard red rubber rectangles arranged in a clamp to rub on the sides of wheel rims. Looking to me like a cross between a Lego brick and a pink school eraser, they stopped us just fine when we squeezed hard on the brake handle mounted on the drop bars but needed to be replaced periodically. One small bicycle headlight provided our nighttime illumination, mounted on the front fork with a friction roller on the side of my tire. This created some drag as it only generated electricity for the tiny bulb when I was moving.

Technology in those days was primitive by today's standards. No cell phones, no GPS, before the Internet, before computers and the information age dominated the culture. Digitized information and GPS mapping capabilities were nonexistent, as was the world wide web. The internet was strictly a military device; by the 1970s some universities were experimenting with internal computer communication from remote sites, but that was barely accessible to the general public. Our location devices were paper maps, pamphlets, and locals who did their best to direct us when we got lost.

Paul's camera, a Nikon F Photomic FTn from 1968, did not come with a phone attached. He bought rolls of Kodak Ektacolor 35mm film in drugstores or camera shops along the way. We had no batteries, no chargers or cables to carry; we never worried about recharging anything except our energy, of course.

Communication Differences. We made the trip before blogs or Instagram existed. The term "social media" wasn't even in our vocabulary until the 1990s. Communication with people who knew we were traveling was dependent on mail (we mailed lots of postcards, we periodically picked up letters from home at General Delivery in post offices where we planned to stop). I sent an occasional hand-written dispatch (by mail) to the Santa Barbara News Press bicycling column editor to let our friends know we were still on the road.

The phone booths we used to stay in touch with the folks back home were the only available means of contact when one was "mobile." You know, the kind that Superman used for changing into his hero suit and cape. We'd drop a dime into the slot on the pay phone and speak to an operator to place a collect call home.

Fancy bicycling attire was not an option, there was no stretchy fabric or flexible, moisture wicking bicycle-specific clothing to keep you comfortable while riding. We looked over our favorite shirts, shorts, and jackets to choose easy to pack, convenient pieces to wear. In Minnesota we fashioned our own convertible pants-to-shorts idea, which we probably should have patented. We gave no thought to bicycle gloves. No specialized shoes, our old canvas sneakers worked. Helmets were strictly for motorcyclists (think Peter Fonda and Dennis Hopper in "Easy Rider").

Freeze-dried food was at an experimental stage in the 1970s and had no flavor unless you enjoyed chewy cardboard. Our camp plates and cups that served as cereal/soup bowls, were made of melamine because plastic was not so prevalent, especially for eating utensils. Two foldable metal fork/spoons came inside our aluminum cook pot set.

ATMs did not exist, so the $1,500 we carried with us was in traveler's checks, wrapped in a waterproof envelope at the bottom of our packs. We figured on a budget of $50 per week, and we stuck to that as much as we could. That covered food shopping, campground fees, the occasional hotel room, and a few bicycle parts. Charge cards were uncommon back then, and it wasn't until October of 1974 that the Equal Opportunity Credit Act would even allow women (me) to acquire one, so bringing along a credit card was not an option. We went with what we had, and figured out the details as they arose.

Why We Ride. When we spotted that poster for BikeCentennial '76, we found the answer—this would be our chance to begin our quest for freedom and adventure. To connect with like-minded bike riders who knew the thrill of riding. Bicycling across the country set us solidly on our path to a no-car lifestyle, our concern for the environment, our connection with nature. Our way to make a statement. Now, in the face of climate change, we are still certain that biking is the way to go.

The small group of inspired individuals who got together to organize BikeCentennial stuck with their plan, and in 1976 somewhere around 4,000 bicyclists traversed the continent on the pre-planned transcontinental bicycle route between Astoria, Oregon, and Yorktown, Virginia. The concept was unique at that time and captured the imagination of countless riders. The organization till exists today as the Adventure Cycling Association. They continue to inspire riders worldwide by providing routes, maps, planned tours, as well as camaraderie and support for anyone looking for an adventure. You can connect with them to find your next adventure at:

https://www.adventurecycling.org/

3  COAST

California . Oregon

Golden Gate Park was our first touchdown as we entered sunny San Francisco. The park stretched for three miles, with acres of emerald rolling lawns, shaded meadows and gardens. I wanted to just hug the ground when we dismounted. Since I had first visited as a teen, the city had been a special place to me—a cosmopolitan gem filled with surprises. When I got a job after high school I'd save part of my paycheck to buy a bus ticket so I could spend a few precious days or a weekend, the Flower Child in me tripping along with free-spirited hippies hanging in the park and Haight Ashbury. Here I was again, after a week of bicycling adventures with my new husband, in San Francisco at last. Standing by my beautiful green 10-speed, a testament that I had pedaled every mile to this spot, I was overwhelmed. Pleased. Thrilled. Proud. The pack-laden bikes fell over onto the soft grass, so we took the cue and plopped ourselves down beside them and stretched out, soaking up the sun and basking in the sense of accomplishment.

The dramatic setting of the San Francisco peninsula with its seven hills—Telegraph Hill, Nob Hill, Russian Hill, Rincon Hill, Twin Peaks, Mount Sutro and Mount Davidson—also includes valleys, inlets, islands, harbors, and beaches. These landforms were shaped millions of years ago by tectonic activity where the San Andreas Fault zone brought together the North American and Pacific continental plates. Geologic uplift and downthrust created the unique energy that attracts a million residents and countless visitors to the City by the Bay, including two transcontinental cyclists.

Journal Entry ~ June 18, 1974 Sleeping late at the Grant Hotel. The bicycles are on the third floor resting with us. Some places are just too good to ride through fast. We'll spend another night here in San Francisco. Yesterday when we arrived, bikes still loaded, we took a quick spin around the city, through the Financial District and North Beach. Sun and wind and memories swirled around with the traffic, we are excited to explore more today. It's just starting to thunder out. Looking over Telegraph Hill the earth above and below appears grey as the fog rolls in, an integral part of the atmosphere here. Across the water in the bay, a circle of silver is shining where the rays of sun rest just before setting. The entire world is looking silvery to me today.

We had our own familiar haunts and secret places, and I even knew of a few back-door entries to some of the popular tourist attractions. We covered every inch on foot or cable cars even though most of the two days and nights we spent in the city it rained. We had toughened up over the last nine days of living outdoors but we'd be walking, first because we could see more that way, and the cable cars would take us everywhere for a quarter. Riding a bike in San Francisco is not the best. It's *hilly*. And *crazy with traffic*. After a short, short nap we were ready for a walk. A quick look out the window of our hotel room told me it was raining. Quite a change from the sound of water pelting the tent.

"Wasn't it a good thing we rode all the way in yesterday?" Paul remarked.

I nodded, grinning, "Now where shall we go?"

"Okay, I'm starving. Been looking forward to dinner at Sam Wo's for a long time!" Paul jumped up, we grabbed our shoes, and were out the door in a flash. We were ready for the best good-food restaurant in Chinatown. Walking down the steep side of Nob Hill, he asked me, "Do you remember how we ever found this place?"

"Yeah, it was one of the first trips I took here with my friend Deanne, remember? She and I rode the Greyhound Bus from Santa Barbara, and when we got to the station we met some folk musicians and joined them on the Muni to Golden Gate Park. After hanging out for awhile they told us about this cool spot to go for supper. They were the first to introduce me to Edsel, the crazy waiter."

Sam Wo's. It was only a few blocks to Kearny Street and Paul remembered we should turn on Washington to find the restaurant. We opened the narrow glass door and entered through the humid, first-floor kitchen. Sounds of clanging pots and kettles, sizzling fat on the grill, shouts in unfamiliar Chinese phrases assaulted us. Squeezing past three stoves crowded with cauldrons of boiling cabbages and noodles, we smiled at the sweaty cooks wielding giant cleavers at the chopping block and headed up narrow stairs to the cramped third floor. Hoping for a couple of empty stools in the galley-like dining room, we scanned the tables and chose two spots near the front window overlooking Washington Street. The air was thick with the salty scent of fried noodles and exotic spice.

"Sit, sit! Find seat!" yelled the legendary rude Chinese waiter. Edsel Fong presided over his tiny domain, playing the role of boss man and entertainer. His manner was mean and blustery, but the twinkle in his eyes gave away the character under the façade.

"What you want?" he barked.

Paul ordered for us. "Two bowls of chow mein. Soft noodles, and two Cokes, please."

"NOPE. Nope. No Cokes!" came the sharp reply. "You want Coke? Across street. No Coke here."

I just smiled and said, "I'll have hot tea." I wasn't in a mood to argue with the angry lord of the dining room.

Paul asked once more, politely, "What soft drinks do you have, then?"

Edsel's face was turning red as he pulled a dollar bill from his apron pocket, slamming it down on the table in front of my husband.

"Shut up! You go across street. You want Coke, I don't have Coke. You go buy your own!" He threw his hands up, pointed out the window at a convenience store. He walked away wiping his hands on his stained white apron, muttering, and shaking his head. We were cracking up.

Deep bowls of rice, chow mein, and stir-fried soft noodles did not disappoint. Chopsticks were the only utensils. We slurped down our tasty, satisfying supper.

"I'm so glad we know about this place," I said. "It's always going to be my favorite spot in San Francisco!"

Later we headed to the Ghirardelli Chocolate Factory for desserts and ice cream sodas. Evenings glowed with colorful neon signs and bright lights, throngs of people chattering on the sidewalks. It was a different scene here, but for us it was a grand celebration. San Francisco—325 miles north of our starting point—was the farthest either of us had ever ridden. I swelled inside now that I knew the answer to the unspoken question, whether we would make it that far and still be in good shape. We ate a lot and spent some of our carefully guarded traveler's checks, saw the sights and ate some more. We enjoyed hot showers at night and real pillows under our heads.

Across the Golden Gate. Great steel cables flashed orange overhead as we cruised over the Golden Gate Bridge. After two days of rest and recuperation we left the city behind and, symbolically, our familiar Southern California home. I wrenched myself away, looking back over my shoulder for practically the entire length of the bridge. For a few uncomfortable hours a void dampened my enthusiasm. The previous 9 days I'd been looking ahead to the joy of reaching San Francisco; this was the first day of uncharted, unknown territory. We got lost, got wet, and felt the chill in the afternoon fog. I wasn't sure at that point where our next milestone would be.

We were heading for Samuel P. Taylor State Park for the night. Finally we found it, set in a serene river valley with towns dotting the coastline and lots of farmland. The mood was a complete contrast to the fast-paced vibe of San Francisco. Nature took sympathy on us and our slight depression that night and provided a cozy spot to sleep in the towering cathedral of Coast Redwoods.

Questions loomed after leaving the familiar city behind. Were we really prepared to continue on, to complete this cross-country trip? We walked among the graceful trees and soft ferns in the early evening and talked about the peace we both found in the calmness of trees, the reassuring steady flow of rivers, in the company of each other. We had something more to build on now that we were entering into new terrain. That thought made me feel much better about the trip and the future. Trees do something special for the wandering soul, showing in their steady permanence that life is good.

Just north of San Francisco we discovered tasty wild huckleberries and juicy pink salmonberries along the roadside in one of the parks. Paul promptly became addicted, and we fought the birds and squirrels for them by the handfuls. We rode through Bodega Bay, the site of Alfred Hitchcock's film "The Birds." The architecture was recognizable—it wasn't too spooky—at least until we noted the skeletons of boats that had washed ashore during storms and left to decay in the little harbor.

California Biking. While hanging out in the company of redwoods, cradled in the softness and silence of the forest, we ran into a handful of bicyclists from all over the country. We shared camp with a couple of guys from St. Louis, then a rider from back east on his way to Vancouver. That guy met his friend from San Francisco at our camp. We talked to a couple on touring bikes who were taking a slow cruise from Redding to San Francisco. There was a group of seven strong, agile cyclists who had come down from Portland. We also spoke to a young woman with a long, flowing ponytail wearing a wrap skirt and crop top, biking on her own, who regaled us with stories about picking wild strawberries and catching a butterfly. Later, outside a grocery store, we met a 10-year-old fellow on his shiny Schwinn Stingray who thoroughly checked out our bikes and gear. He then declared that, although he had always lived in the nearby town where he was born, he planned to leave as soon as he grew up! Bikers from all walks of life, sharing the wanderlust.

Journal Entry ~ June 20, 1974 We're sitting in a little creek bed having lunch, surrounded by redwoods and ferns a little distance from the road, close to the ocean. Tree trunks are rooted on the slope below street level at the bottom of this creek and stretch straight up, hundreds of feet above us, reaching for the sun. Oblivious to the traffic on the highway, they thrive in the damp earth; young trees are fed by decaying trunks of fallen ancients, and a delicate undergrowth of smaller plants supports and nurtures the forest in a special symbiosis to create these giant redwoods.

Reluctant to leave the special beauty of the redwood coast, we decided to camp and explore as many parks, streams, and beach spots as we could. Salt Point campground was full, but the ranger took pity on our plight; he saw that we had been fighting headwinds and had no energy to go further. He directed us out of the park to a secluded grassy area called Marine Mesa, which he described as an ancient sea bottom. The wind blasted that ancient sea bottom all night, we had our tent corners propped up and tied to our leaning bicycles in some impossible configuration. At least we slept okay. The next day, moving slowly—more for the scenery than from wind—we explored Sea Ranch and checked out the lighthouse at Point Arena where great rough waves thundered into the rocky beachhead at the point.

When we reached Van Damme State Park, we were ready for another day of exploration. After we cleaned our clothes and showered at the park facilities, we set up our camp facing a bend in the river trickling through a fern canyon thick with the branching arms of sword ferns. The next morning dawned still and clear, so we explored more trails and ocean views before heading north to the next town. Mendocino was a charming coastal city, decorated with Victorian style homes on the cliffs above the ocean, and cypress trees posed in picturesque shapes along the rocky shore. My favorite photographer was in his element and spent hours shooting photos, steadying the Nikon camera on fence posts to capture the incredible scenery.

Fort Bragg. The next morning we found ourselves in Fort Bragg and decided to take a detour up Woody Rd. to explore a huge greenhouse Paul had spotted. What at first appeared to be acres of green grass on platforms turned out to be about a million baby pine trees. Superintendent Amy Thompson took us through the humid, plastic-covered tunnel while she explained how she cared for the redwood and Douglas fir seedlings. Each container protected the root plugs; she watered, fertilized, and tested the foliage while giving them lots of TLC. Paul was spellbound and could have stayed right there in the nursery to help nurture those babies—more baby trees than he had ever seen. The Georgia Pacific Lumber Company had begun the experimental tree farm to replace trees used in the logging industry. That crop would be ready to plant in October, right around the same time our trip would be over. In another 50 years they would be ready for harvest.

Avenue of the Giants. Pulling off the main Coast Highway, we leaned into the gentle curves of the scenic road that took us through the tallest stands of trees in Humboldt Redwoods State Park. Ancient old growth forest giants hundreds and sometimes thousands of years old surrounded us. Impossibly huge trees to the left, right, straight ahead, and up; I stretched my head back to see the tops that towered overhead with spires some 30 stories above me and my tiny bike. The blue sky was nearly invisible through thick evergreen branches, the trunks making cathedrals in the feathery light that filtered down upon the forest floor. I joyfully coasted through the cool, moist air scented with spicy redwood bark. These amazing trees, *Sequoia semperverins*, thrive along California's coastal ranges for several hundred miles. The conjunction of fog, moisture, cliffs, beach, and mountains created a unique environment for these exquisite redwood giants. Throughout this state park we drifted for over 30 miles, pedaling deep in the woods, leafy ferns blanketing the forest floor while Stellar's blue jays flitted past, their chatter echoing around the columns of trees.

Journal Entry ~ June 26, 1974 *Yellow flower carpet falls from the hills to the edge of this rocky beach. We're 15 or 20 miles north of Fort Bragg. Sun shining and shorts on. The headwinds have, for the time being, subsided. Logging trucks are now part of our daily experience—pretty frightening to a bicyclist. But there are no double-trailer trucks and, so far, all that pass give us more consideration than many other motorists.*

Breakdown. We were having a beautiful ride along the sea and had just stopped for a break when we met another biker coming toward us. We exchanged hellos, and he stopped for a brief rest on the rocks where we sat.

"How's the road up ahead?" Paul wanted to know.

"You're headed that way? I feel sorry for you!"

"What is it, a hill?"

"I just came over the biggest, or at least longest hill since Olympia, Washington! Coming from the other way it's not so bad, but I must have just coasted down about 9 miles—and it's steep!"

With that bit of encouragement, we gathered up our gear and figured we'd better tackle it. Paul and I weren't yet seasoned hill climbers, only 3 weeks and 500 miles into our trip. We had hopes of riding to the East Coast. That would involve crossing the Rockies and the Continental Divide. The hills and slopes so far had been manageable. Now the question was in front of us: *Can we actually ride up a 9-mile hill?*

The road turned inland; in less than a mile we were deep in tall shady forest trees. It was beautiful, and cool, and such a change that we barely noticed the little bit of climbing we were doing.

I could hear Paul call over his shoulder to me. "This is some really beautiful country! These trees have been growing here for a good long time."

"Maybe this hill isn't going to be as bad as we thought. At least it will be worth it. And I'm glad it's so much cooler... What's that noise you're making, anyway?" I could hear a creaking as he pedaled.

"Just that same old annoying part. The cotter pin is probably loose again." Paul—always the confident, optimistic rider.

"Hey, here come some more bikes...Hey hello...is it very much farther up?"

The three sailed past us, too fast on the downhill to even hear us. But we caught that, yes, it was pretty far to the top.

The hill was getting steeper now. Paul's bike was making loud clunking noises and we'd just shifted almost simultaneously into first gear. Another log truck came grinding by. We were navigating tight "U" shaped turns, like switchbacks on a challenging hiking trail.

"I'm going to stop and tighten this down, Lynn. You can ride on and I'll catch up."

I normally wouldn't ride out ahead of him, but we were on a steep grade and I didn't want to lose momentum. I knew we needed to encourage one another to make it up the hills. I rode slowly ahead but stopped a little way up to wait for him so we could ride together.

"Okay...go ahead!" I heard him call. I pushed off and glanced over my shoulder to see him mount up.

After a minute, I heard a log truck rumbling from around the curve behind the trees. After all our weeks of riding our hearing, judging, balancing senses were heightened. We were continuously recording things almost at the subconscious level—an important factor in making decisions as we rode in tight circumstances.

A sudden sound of metal scraping, leaves, gravel, and dirt moving alarmed me. I hit the brakes and turned to see Paul lying horizontal, feet still locked in the toe clips. A 40-ton loaded log truck sailed past him and around the sharp curve.

For a half second, icy cold fright sliced through my heart. *Had he been hit? Did he break something in the fall?* I could not tell what had happened. To steady myself from the panic, I planted my feet on the ground, swung my bike around toward oncoming traffic, and headed back downhill—trying not to fear the worst—that couple of seconds seemed to go on forever.

I was still shaky by the time I reached him, but he was getting up and off his bike. I could see the busted crank was what toppled him, the too-close log truck was just a coincidence. Thankfully, he had fallen *after* the truck went by. We assessed the damage: a scraped knee and a broken bicycle crank. This was clearly worse for the bike than for Paul.

Hitch A Ride. A stand of trees offered shade alongside the road where Paul took apart the crank to inspect the damage. The cone inside the bearing cage had broken and disintegrated the bearings. He tried wire and ingenuity in the place of spare parts. I pulled out a salami and some carrots to nibble on, and we laughed a little at his $89 department-store bike—the Batavus Special—and how many miles he had actually put on it before anything broke. We wouldn't have to ride the rest of the hill now, but we had a different sort of challenge.

"Well, we can't go anywhere now, not on this bike." Paul was thinking of our next move.

"What if we can't get the piece you need in the next town? It's a pretty small place." In my mind, I was asking deeper questions. Like, what if our bikes keep breaking down? Paul had already had a couple of flats. We had a few tools to fix things and make adjustments. But parts...what about those? I was counting on Paul to be the mechanic. Did I expect him to be able to supply us with anything we needed? How could he? And there was so much more of the continent to cover!

"At least we're close to somewhere civilized today." I knew there would be miles of open country in Wyoming and South Dakota where we wouldn't see anybody, let alone a bicycle shop. I was silently questioning our sanity: we had traveled this far and I was more than a little worried about what we were going to do.

In the next few hours I learned first-hand what you do when a broken bike interrupts a cross-country tour: you fix the bike and move on! In this case we experienced so much more, meeting friendly people willing to come to our aid.

First, we got a ride from a vacationing family over that big hill to the campground at Standish Hickey State Park where we were headed for the night. The rangers chuckled a little as we limped the bike into camp.

"Do you know of any bike stores near here?"

"Not around here. No stores, except if you count the post office. Not until you get to Ukiah." Ukiah was 60 miles south on the Interstate—bicycles prohibited on that highway.

The picnic table that night was spread not with camp stove and hot dinner, but the innards and broken parts of Paul's bicycle. With the help of the rangers, we sought out all possibilities of another 10-speed around with a replacement part we could beg, borrow, or steal. Not a one to be found. Eventually, we shared camp with three other transcontinental bike tourers, one all the way from Connecticut. None of them, understandably, would part with their own bearing cone and they didn't have any spare parts with them. We got lots of sympathy, and good company, but no fixed bike.

"Looks like tomorrow's lost to hitchhiking."

"Yeah, but at least we got this far with no hassles. How long do you think it'll take to get 120 miles round-trip?"

"I don't know, we don't even know if Ukiah has a bike store. But we'll have to find out."

The rangers in the park were quite accommodating. They let us keep our bikes and gear in an old shed for the day. With just our thumbs and the piece Paul needed to replace, we got a ride all the way to the town early the next morning.

Ukiah Hike. We checked at service stations with no luck. In the corner phone booth we looked up two bike stores—both were at the other end of town from where we were. Ukiah was one of those long, narrow communities that stretched out for miles down one main street. We were on foot and had to hike three miles before we found the store. The first one didn't have the piece to fit his bike. Disappointed, we walked another mile or so and, finally, we were in luck!

"It's tough to be walking, we could have made this distance in no time on the bicycles. And besides, we can't even say we're on a cross-country bike trip if we don't even have the bikes with us!" We were both feeling a bit lost and out of our element.

With the aid of helpful motorists, rangers, and friendly shopkeepers, we accomplished what we had come for. Maybe our sense of independence was bruised, but I had learned that in this kind of emergency we were equipped to deal with problems we encountered. Even without the bike to ride, we had our camp gear, food, supplies, and the good earth to sleep on. We could have waited and even figured the bike part could be shipped to the park if we'd had to. It was another learning experience. People were always willing to lend a good-natured hand.

The day was successful. We hitched a ride in a truck back to the state park near Fort Bragg–but not before gorging ourselves at a smorgasbord in Ukiah. All-you-can-eat Salisbury steak, potatoes, gravy, and steamed vegetables. Dessert was a treat after our day's trials, and the whole thing cost only $2.00 apiece. The bike was fixed and we had a good night at camp. Our spirits were lifted and we awoke anxious to be on our way, with added confidence in ourselves and the fantastic folk all around us.

Journal Entry ~ June 30, 1974 Wind was blowing hard as we rode along the high grassy sand dunes at Clam Beach this afternoon. We've decided to stay here to camp in a rather unofficial spot right along the beach. We put our bikes and packs out of sight, hiding among the sea grass, and the beach is nearby. No one should notice we're here. The walk down to the water below the cliff is not too steep, and so we're just watching the waves crashing and feeling the salty mist blowing off the churning white water. Paul found a perfect piece of driftwood and carved me a fork for cooking and turning food in our little frying pan. It's beautiful, and more than a souvenir, but a functional utensil we'll use every day.

Samoa Cookhouse. More food than we had ever seen, in Eureka, California, at the lumberjack restaurant in Samoa. The red wooden barn structure definitely had the look of a company cookhouse—long, low rooftop, a wall of windows, and a big Welcome sign at the door on the end. Ranch-style tables draped in red-checkered cloths and benches stretched out in long rows. Among the crowded, communal seating, we found space at the end of one table and food began to appear on trays, family style all-you-can-eat. The food was hearty, hot, and filling. But the best part was when the servers brought whole pies to the table, as many as we wanted—apple, pecan, blueberry, mixed berries—and buckets of whipped cream or ice cream to top it off. After a couple of hours of gobbling, just one more slice of pie, please, we were reluctant to leave but we still had more riding to do that day.

Oregon State Border. We left Crescent City, California, behind and for several miles there wasn't much in the way of population or signs of civilization. We were about to cross the border into our next state. The first time in the history of our bicycles that this had been done. Neither of us had ever been to Oregon. I was looking for the border line across the road.

"How will we know when we cross into Oregon?"

"You'll know when we get there," was the only response I got from Paul. He usually was not very vocal, but always ready with a sense of humor.

A little further up the road I saw the carved cedar sign that spelled out OREGON. Paul pointed out the California State border check on the other side of the street. It was a little like leaving a friend behind, my home for all the years I could remember. But if I was going to get that sentimental, what was I doing on this trip, anyway?

So I focused on our present accomplishment. "Hey, it feels different here, doesn't it? Already the license plates are different." Naturally, the first thing we met in Oregon was a hill. But the roads were wide and clean, and we noticed that was the case almost all the way through the state.

"You can ride anywhere in Oregon without getting off a freeway. We have one of the best freeway systems anywhere," a waitress told us later. Since we were into our second state, I wanted lunch! After all, it was 1:30 when we got to the border and I get hungrier when I'm excited.

"Good. You find us a place out of the wind, and we'll have something to eat." Paul snapped.

One thing in common between California and Oregon coastlines—you will rarely find a place "out of the wind." Crossing the first state border seemed to strain the emotions. There was a little friction building between us as my hunger took over and made me more frustrated. Luckily we heard about a state park a few miles up the road and decided to head there to eat and maybe stop for the day.

The remarkable feature we found at parks in southern Oregon—electric stoves in campgrounds. At each spot we stopped there were coin-operated cooking facilities under wood-covered picnic areas. We figured the abundance of moisture made electric cooking the most economical. Here, it seemed, the national energy crisis of the 1970s was not so bad. We saved spending money on a couple of cans of gas fuel for our little stove.

We settled in for lunch but realized that the forested park was going to be damp all night. We slept under the stars on a fiberglass picnic table, me on the bench and Paul on the table—we thought the tent might fill with moisture if it rained. The humidity formed a thick wet fog hugging our sleeping bags. At least it hadn't rained...yet.

Seven Devils Road. In Coos County Forest we followed a rural route along Seven Devils Road—a windy and forsaken path.

"Why did we come this way anyhow?" I was feeling the desolation along the deserted, twisting road.

"It will save us more than 5 miles this way. We can get to Coos Bay in time to get our mail from home at General Delivery before the post office closes."

"We haven't seen a car for the last two hours. Do you think this road goes anywhere at all?" I was not having any fun.

Signs along the edge of road warned against trespassing or berry picking. The name of the road—Seven Devils—set the mood. Ominous clouds closed in, graying up my already dark mindset. This day seemed to go on forever and I was not exactly sure where we would end up, or if we'd have to stop somewhere along the roadside to camp: no shelter from the storm! It was unsettling when I considered the situation we were in.

"It looks like it's gonna pour any minute now. Are we too far to go back the other way?"

The sky turned a steely gray and cold rain splashed down on our backs and shoulders. Wind blew us ahead of the storm at about 20 miles an hour. We wore shorts to preserve the long pants for nighttime, knowing shorts allowed much more free movement than tight, soggy jeans would have. The uphills seemed never-ending as I put my head down, one pedal turn after another, drenched inside from sweat and outside from rain. Then, riding down the hills—raindrops flying in my face, dripping down my nose, I had little confidence that brakes would work on the slick pavement. I simply tensed up and slid recklessly downhill until the road leveled off. This was more exhausting than dry riding. We usually didn't last too many hours in the rain, but on this windy day we covered 50 miles.

Finally we made it into Charleston, Oregon. There we were, in front of one of those seedy-looking trailer parks that begrudgingly rent spaces to "overnighters." We pulled into a coffee shop for a break to think it over. Indoors and warm, we decided on the lesser of two evils. We needed a place to stay and we didn't want to go any further to find it. So we went back, plunked down our $3.50 plus a $1 deposit on the restroom/laundry key, and set up camp between puddles. At least the guy was good enough to give us a site with two trees for our tent-pitching. Supper was about ready, and it started to rain.

"Quick, grab those pots and get inside the tent," I shouted over the drumming of the rain.

"You cover the bikes up, and I'll pull in the sleeping bags," Paul answered.

We just made it inside, and the pelting began.

That downpour lasted until we finished eating—with the promise of more as the night settled in. One more trip to the restrooms, trading off the keys. The restroom was at the back of a small laundry room with a couple of rusted washers and dryers and a Coke machine. It didn't take long for sleep to descend that night. With hopes of dispelling the day's misery in sweet dreams, we settled in.

DRIP, DRIP, DRIP...

"Are you awake?" I knew he was awake.

DRIP, SPLASH, SPLASH...

"Yeah..."

"What do we do now? Can't stay in here much longer...."

"I have this edge of the tent protected by the Frisbee, but water is coming up anyway."

The steady gush of water outside muffled our groaning and grumbling. We considered knocking on somebody's trailer to beg refuge, but it was already midnight.

"Okay, that's it. My sleeping bag is under water. Let's get out of here."

"Shall we try the laundry room...do you think they'd care?"

"I don't CARE if they care—just get going."

In stocking-feet I threw my sleeping bag over my head and shoulders, foolishly thinking that would protect me—then sploosh, squish, the puddles were ankle deep—and the whole camp was one great big pond.

We decided who got the floor, and who got the one-foot-wide bench on the premise that Paul couldn't sleep on cold hard surfaces without a pillow. I tried sitting up and leaning on the soda machine to stay off the damp concrete, but eventually ended up curled into a fetal position under my soaked sleeping bag on the floor. After an hour or two of sleep, we sloshed our things together into a bundle, piled everything on the bike racks, and headed for town. We found a larger, cheaper laundromat that was open, so we took the tent and sleeping bags and all the clothes we didn't need to wear and filled dryer after dryer, feeding dimes into the machines.

Shortly, another biker came rolling down the hill. Wet as we had been. He had camped even further up Seven Devils, on the beach with another group of riders. We eventually met all of them: 15 kids from a high school class and their teacher—with their accompanying water-logged high school gym clothes, tents, and sleeping bags. A crazy rainbow splash of camp-gear colors strapped to their bikes, the crowd of riders tucked in under the overhanging roof cover at the front of the tiny laundromat.

Two ladies were doing laundry early when we got there. They were gone within minutes as the whole troupe of wet and irritated bikers filed in and took over. As the local women left, they informed us good-naturedly that in Oregon "you don't tan, you rust." This was the middle of summer, and it was sure rusty out.

We waited on the dryers while the hungry teens dipped into two gallons of milk and cereal. Paul and I polished off our own quart and two dozen mini-donuts from the nearby market when it finally opened.

Hosteling. This was not to be our last bout with awful days and rougher nights in Coos County. Paul was blessed with another flat tire. He'd gone through five flats already and we were sick of it. So next on the agenda was a good new tire. Coos Bay Post Office had mail for us at General Delivery, and we bought fried chicken for lunch to restore our spirits. And still it rained. There was a bike store that had what we needed, once again at the far end of town. We got the tire and by 1:00, wiped out from the lack of sleep in the restroom-laundromat, we started looking for places to stay. Asking around, we found that Coos Bay had a hostel set up in a church basement. It was not the best of accommodations, but I argued that it was at least better than sleeping outdoors. I was desperate for some sleep. Our tent had become our cozy honeymoon home, so we were surprised to learn that the hostel had separate sleeping rooms for men and women. No fun, and not comfortable sleeping on the floor, but at least it was dry. Again, morning came too early.

"Knock! Knock! Knock! It's Morning. Rise and Shine. Rise and Shine!"

Stumbling upstairs, we were all looking for coffee, but the director of the establishment had been up way before us and he wanted the floors swept and furniture moved before we left. I took the kitchen cleanup duty, Paul went through the motions of sweeping floors. We left quickly and swore off hosteling from then on.

Furthest West Point. "Paul. Is this worth 5 extra miles—a 10-mile round trip—for you just to see this 'furthest West point'?" I was skeptical.

"Well, yes. It really is something, you know. The whole country to cross—this will be the actual start of our ride East, see. Besides, the wind isn't bad now, and it will be behind us. C'mon. You'll only be here once!"

A woman in the visitor center at the border had mentioned this campground, and that Cape Blanco was indeed the westernmost point of land on the continental United States. I figured Paul was just as concerned as I was about going miles out of our way for no reason. This milestone seemed to be worthwhile to him, and it would at least provide a place to camp for the night, so I followed. Happily, we found soft grass to camp on, free firewood, and a nice shower facility. After dinner, just at sunset, we locked the bikes and walked beyond the campground to the point of land jutting out to the ocean. A beautiful lighthouse guarded the rocky shore. We soaked in the crimson red glow of the sunset, and then the silence of dusk.

Turning toward the east, Paul stretched his arms out. "You can almost see the whole country laid out right in front of us...just waiting for us to ride across." His enthusiasm overflowed.

That thought brought me around to appreciate Paul's insistence on stopping, and I began to recognize what sorts of things were important to him.

"Just think of all the places between here and there and how much we'll ride through. What's straight east of here on the Atlantic, do you know?" I asked.

"Probably just about where we're headed. Maybe a little farther north," he guessed. When we checked on a map later it turned out to be just a few miles north of Cape Cod on a straight line.

We embraced there on the cliff, with the Pacific Ocean view surrounding us on three sides out on the point, thoughts so far in the future of the next two months we couldn't even imagine them. A bubble as big as the sea, as broad as the expanse of land ahead, swelled inside me as I held on tight to my best biking partner. Then suddenly we remembered the bikes and hurried back to camp—there wouldn't be a chance of crossing any country if anything happened to our four wheels.

Images flashed by in the rain the next day, breaking up the showers—fence posts, leaning mailboxes, pinecones on the ground, spruce tree branches waving overhead. Even under these damp conditions we were seeing new sights and being rewarded for our efforts. On a Sunday morning, before it rained too hard, a woman in a bright orange robe was out in her yard getting the newspaper. She waved to us.

"Good morning. Having a nice ride? Enjoy your day!"

Then, from a gentleman on his porch on the other side of the road, "Hey—where ya headed? Looks like a lot of fun."

All the Oregonians we met made us feel like we were being welcomed. Later, after several hours of pedaling diligently in chilly rain, we were even offered a ride. Paul spoke to the family in the van that stopped to see if they could give us a lift. He turned them down. "We want to do this on the bikes, right?" I had to agree, even though the warm, dry van looked awfully tempting.

At Lincoln City we turned east, away from the headwinds—leaving the ocean behind. This was the northernmost spot we'd see on the coastline and soon we would reach 1000 miles. We stopped along the road and changed from long pants into shorts and warm-weather t-shirts. Now that we were inland, away from the exasperating sea breezes, we felt the summer sun.

Journal Entry ~ July 12, 1974 I am a bike rider, only one body, a small speck of energy in the universe, privileged to be doing this trip. Laying here in sunshine after having covered 1000 miles on my awesome bike, I see every moment as a sparkle that's become a part of me. I only hope I can find a way to share this new energy, beyond myself. If I can remain open and become an instrument to collect all the small unknown experiences as I ride and offer them for other people to enjoy, then maybe I will have grasped the greatest thing life has to offer—connection with others. I am too full to keep it inside—it will have to come out somehow!

At the 1,000-mile point, we were ready to celebrate—even though it was just another mile along the road. July 12, and 34 days after our start, we stretched out on the grass at our camp and tried to absorb this incredible moment. My heart was full, and completely in the moment, in the middle of a wide, wide continent I was getting to know—one mile at a time.

We tracked mileage from the distances marked on our maps. Paul recorded daily point-to-point miles and added them up in a little notebook he carried. To our delight we spotted a roadside park right about where we wanted to stop and congratulate ourselves. It was in a place called Van Duzer Corridor, a low pass between the mountain range and forested hills. Coincidentally, we were not far from having crossed the 45th Parallel outside of Lincoln City. There we were, tripping along on the surface of the globe halfway between the equator and the North Pole. Paul pulled out a roll of Lifesavers he'd tucked down into one of the packs the day we left, a little memento from our last day in Santa Barbara. We toasted the next three thousand miles ahead of us with sweet candies, anticipating what wonders the rest of the ride would bring.

McMinnville. About 40 miles before Portland, we stopped in McMinnville where we saw a carnival, a parade, and preparation for a bicycle race in celebration of TurkeyRama. At first we thought, of course, the celebration was all about us. We asked where the bike shop was and someone directed us to Tommy's Hobby and Bike Store. Their knowledgeable mechanic, Al, helped us out with a sticky crank on my bike that he found was simply clogged with dirt and mud. Then we asked about a place to camp for the night and he called out to the owner.

Tommy was jovial and friendly. "You're just looking for a place for the night? Got a tent? Well, then, come over to our house, we'll fix you up. We've got food and a shower if you like, too."

A grin stole over my face as I exchanged looks with my husband. Now, let's try not to jump over the counter with enthusiasm and kiss the guy. After the awful rainy days we'd just had, we were so ready for someone to ask us into their home.

"Are you sure it's all right? We wouldn't be in the way?" I asked.

"Nope, are you kidding? We'd love to have you. And then maybe you'll do the same for us. We are planning to go bicycle touring someday, too, you know." His eyes were sparkling, and sincere, and we were so grateful.

We met Tommy's wife and three children and set up camp in their backyard. After a delicious dinner we talked bikes and touring and shared stories of our ride. Their daughter, 8-year-old Mona, explained about the Turkey Festival. Apparently, McMinnville, which is in the heart of the fertile Willamette Valley, was once a turkey farm area, and each summer they had a fair, served turkey, and held turkey races. Since there weren't many turkey ranches around anymore, Tommy turned the turkey race into a bicycle race, with local businesses competing for a trophy.

On Saturday morning, Portland beckoned but we decided to stay in McMinnville to see the race. Paul rode along in Tommy's truck to help mark the course. We took our leave, just after everyone had begun the first lap around, and planned to make Portland by evening.

After a good night's rest in a small hotel, we caught Portland sleeping early in the morning. The city was quiet, peaceful, and every store was closed. We got a greasy, tasty breakfast at a place called Fogleman's Burger and Omelette Emporium where we spent an hour catching up in the journals over coffee.

"Hey, let's see what this scale has to say," Paul suggested when he noticed the old green steel penny-scale contraption in front of the drugstore on the corner. Dropping our nickels into the slot, we faced the awful truth.

"Hold my bike and I'll weigh myself and then you hand it to me and we'll see what the difference really is," Paul went first.

"Just me is 175 pounds. Me and the bike, 257 pounds. Ugh! Wow, you try it."

I struggled to stand upright holding the bike fully loaded, but weighed in at 176 altogether, me alone at 112 pounds. We decided we were lugging around too much stuff and actually shed 5 or 10 pounds of nonessential equipment to hopefully lighten the load. Before we left Portland we went through the packs and sent home a few choice items, like a dress I had been foolish enough to bring, Paul's headlight (we slept when it was dark), and an extra shirt and shorts.

Traveling northeast out of town, we were on a quiet road off the main highway, riding through relatively flat farmlands and open space. Suddenly, Paul screeched to a halt.

"Holy Smokes! Look at that!"

I stopped, found where he was looking, and spotted the great cone of snow-dipped Mt. Hood floating like a cloud over the distant horizon, beckoning. The huge volcano loomed above everything else. A part of the Cascade Range, Mt. Hood stayed in our view, and became a landmark for many miles as we continued our eastward route alongside the magnificent Columbia River.

4  Earth Day

2024 Reflections

I can clearly remember the confusion that swirled around me and my bike back then, at the point in Lincoln City when we turned away from the Pacific Coast. I had committed to a transcontinental ride with Paul so of course I knew the inevitability of leaving the ocean behind. Since that time, I've become aware of the profound changes that have occurred along the coast. The world is profoundly changed. I also take advantage of the fact that, these days, I can check the Internet; instant retrospective lies literally at my fingertips. So I cast my attention back to that time, reflecting on how these changes impact me today.

Beach Birds. The beach was always my favorite place to ride and to play. The ocean provided a way of life for me and my brothers. Once I met Paul, he and I spent a lot of time walking barefoot on the shore. Gliding along the California Coast together represents some of the best memories of our entire trip. My bike gave me wings, like a gull surfing the crests of waves, soaring along the cliffs of Big Sur, jays and crows winging like acrobats through the redwoods. The lightness sticks with me, even as the soaring birds I bike with these days on Arizona's high plateau are ravens, hawks, and bald eagles.

I also hold a vivid memory of the day the beaches in my hometown turned black with oil sludge. Walking barefoot in the sand meant I always needed to keep a bottle of baby oil and rags handy to clean the soles of my feet because blobs of crude oil floating in with the surf stuck to the skin. The half-dozen offshore oil rigs on the horizon were unsightly but we tolerated them until that fateful day in January 1969 when one of the drills blew out. A terrible, damaging oil slick floated toward the coastline and coated everything in sight. The air smelled industrial and acrid, ocean-loving birds and fish died and washed up on the beaches.

We wept for the sea life when we saw seagulls strewn across the sand, wings coated in thick sludge, their feathers, feet, and beaks immobilized and caked in black, sticky oil. Everyone in town spent what free time they had tenderly rescuing birds that were still alive and bringing them to the makeshift rescue center near the zoo to be treated. Only some were able to be rehabilitated and released.

First Earth Day. By the next summer, after the alarming devastation of wildlife wrought by an unregulated industry, the nation was inspired to take action. Several events converged to kickstart the environmental movement before our bike trip began. Just months before the spill, astronauts on Apollo 8 had shared the first photographs of Earth from space. The striking effect of seeing those images of our lonely blue ball spinning in the blackness of space gave the world a new perspective of the special, fragile planet we live on.

During that single year 20 million Americans marched for change. In 1970 Earth Day was established, supported by grassroots activists and members of Congress, to celebrate and emphasize our responsibility to care for the earth. Later that year the Environmental Protection Agency (EPA) was created, tasked with protecting the environment and safeguarding the health and well-being of humanity. I remember that first Earth Day in April of 1970 as a personal victory, owned by every beach lover living in Santa Barbara. Paul and I rode our bikes both for fun and for transportation. We joyfully celebrated the birth of environmental awareness.

Casmalia Now. That celebration of hope was on my mind in 1974 when we bicycled through Casmalia and heard about the nearby dump that was causing so much concern. I was inspired to research what happened there. I discovered that the Casmalia Resources Hazardous Waste Landfill was indeed opened in 1973 to store waste from oil companies and agricultural operations. Today I read about the horrific substances it handled: dangerous chemicals, solvents, and pesticides including 40,000 gallons a day of toxic liquid waste from an acid pit. The dump, sitting on the hills above Casmalia, contaminated the soil and groundwater. In the early 1980s, people noticed increases in respiratory ailments and birth defects. Residents protested. Reports described how the local farmers blocked the entrance with hay bales to keep trucks from dumping waste.

The EPA was set up to deal with just this kind of crisis. The Casmalia dump closed in 1989 when it became one the first Superfund sites. (Superfund is an EPA process that requires responsible parties to clean up facilities deemed hazardous to human health and the environment.) Today, fifty years later, Casmalia's population is still relatively small but there is a store, the post office remains open, and a popular restaurant with a long history continues to serve the surrounding communities. Retirees live in town and still enjoy the rural, peaceful atmosphere that Mrs. Granden treasured. The superfund action stands as a sign of the progress we've made since we met her. We could do more, we need to do more. One step at a time, and I count this as moving in the right direction.

More Coastal Memories. One hundred miles north of Casmalia, the Coast Highway begins the climb up to the Big Sur Headlands. The Piedras Blancas Lighthouse sits just south of the start of Big Sur Highway, where we rode those dramatic cliffs, curves, and redwood forests of the coast I hold dear. My very first camping trip up to Big Sur was with Paul the summer before we were married in 1974. We drove in his Red Baron VW and I remember sitting perched on a cliff at the edge of the world, vibrating with the rays of sunset as the choppy surf rolled on the incoming tide, crashing into the rocks far below.

I know a lot more today about Big Sur than I did then. I've learned some of the history of the original Native American tribes who inhabited this amazing coastline, including the Esselen, the Ohlone, and the Salinam. In 2020, a substantial portion of land north of the Little Sur River was returned to members of the Esselen tribe through a conservation grant. Long after Spanish explorers claimed these lands 250 years ago, the fishing and ceremonial grounds are once again under the stewardship of Indigenous peoples. They will be able to restore and conserve these lands following traditional ways with the hope of sharing their culture and lifestyle with others.

Climate Effects. The space where the sea meets the land at the foot of the coastal range traditionally averages 50 inches of rainfall that flows down streams in the Santa Lucia mountains. Big Sur has always attracted weather events. It saddens me to learn how, as the climate shifts in response to the human-caused effects on the planet, changes are affecting the unique and fragile coastal area. Forests weakened by insect infestation are devastated by raging wildfires every summer. Increased rainfall, sudden and intensely heavier these days, causes more flooding, landslides, and rock falls that frequently close Highway 1 along the Big Sur coast.

When we rode that strip of highway five decades ago, the idea of taking a bicycle tour through Big Sur was nothing more than an exciting, exhilarating adventure. Now I read on bicycling blogs that this path is not recommended, impossible to traverse due to increased traffic, often closed for months at a time while highway crews constantly work repairing and restoring the narrow paved sections on the edge of cliffs that have broken loose and fallen into the sea. I know of several long-distance riders who had planned to make Big Sur part of their journey but were unable to complete that section due to two major landslides and a bridge collapse that occurred in the past year. As Caltrans crews worked to clear the debris on the steep cliff, some determined riders have attempted to walk bikes across the construction zone.

Our Stories Continue. Years after our transcontinental tour Paul and I made more memories along the Big Sur headlands. In the 1990s our two children were in their teens and our jobs required us to live inland, in Thousand Oaks and then Simi Valley, California. Paul had kept up his bicycling on weekends, but my work and parenting schedule for many years prevented me from even thinking about recreation or exercise. One day, when he heard of a group ride sponsored by the nonprofit Kiwanis Service Club, he said he'd like to try it. The ride started nearby at the Ventura State Beach Park and followed the coastline up to Santa Barbara. That inspired me and I decided that, if he was going to ride, so was I.

We began training again, riding the same two bikes that had taken us across the country. Eventually we replaced those ten-speeds, but not until we realized that bicycling would always be a part of our lifestyle. We signed up for charity rides every summer after that, making for some great adventures—back on the bicycles, riding along the coast together. Then, in 1999 when I was about to turn 50, we found out the San Luis Obispo Bicycle Club (SLO-BC) held a club ride from San Luis Obispo to the Piedras Blancas Lighthouse. I would pedal 50 miles for my 50th birthday. Granted, it was a struggle in places, but turned into a joyful, exhilarating experience for me. I earned my first commemorative bicycle jersey, patches, and a free lunch. I still have that jersey and wear it when I go out on the e-bike.

Since that time, I've learned more about the importance of physical activity in my maturity. I continue to find freedom and excitement when I ride but, even more, I appreciate the benefits I derive from being outdoors, pushing myself to stay in shape, staying strong. Biking remains one of the highlights of my summer days. Additionally, I catch glimpses all the time of grassroots cycling enthusiasts and activists making progress, making changes, proving to me that bicycling offers unlimited possibilities.

Inspiration. I am inspired by women who ride, women who write, and, naturally, women who do both. You are all heroines to me. A few years ago I discovered Dr. Kate Rawles, a bicycle rider from the U.K. who rode solo on her bicycle 4,553 miles north to south along the Rocky Mountains of North America. I read her book, "The Carbon Cycle," and everything she wrote about resonated strongly with me. I journeyed along with her as I read—inspired by the power of one woman to send such a strong message using bicycling as a vehicle. Her sense of urgency about the state of the planet and concern for the earth shines through. She later followed up on the same theme, communicating her environmental message when she built a bamboo bicycle and completed another ride, along the backbone of South America, and wrote of the journey in "The Life Cycle." You can discover her message for yourself:

https://www.outdoorphilosophy.co.uk/

Our local independent book shop listed another title, "Bicycling with Butterflies," by Sara Dykman. I became captivated early on by the fascinating story of the monarch migration, from the days when we watched the fragile creatures fluttering among the eucalyptus leaves in California. Sara rode her bicycle loaded with packs and gear, retracing the butterflies' path from Mexico to Canada and back. She describes that journey in her book, bringing the plight of butterflies to the attention of the world. She continues to spread the message of saving the butterflies and caring for nature at the educational website she founded:

https://www.beyondabook.org/

Soon after I began work on this book, I had the opportunity to meet Kristen Jokinen, the amazing author of "Joy Ride: A Bike Odyssey from Alaska to Argentina." She and her husband Ville, already seasoned world travelers and adventurers, came to Flagstaff to present the story of their incredible 18,000-mile bikepacking trip. Kristen's enthusiasm and ability to connect with everyone she meets brought back to me the same warmth that Paul and I found when we traveled on our trip—emphasizing the basic friendliness and openness of humankind that they have discovered in countless situations. Kristen's story, her message of hope, and her smile inspired me as I worked through telling my own story. She and her husband are still out there, pedaling the world and keeping in touch at:

https://www.welostthemap.com/

5  RIVERS

Oregon . Idaho . Wyoming

For the first thousand miles we'd been hugging the Pacific Coast where the reassurance of sea breezes and sandy beaches embraced me. The route from here on was unfamiliar. I was feeling curious, but cautious. Would I find the same comfort following alongside rivers? Would they be accessible in their continuous flowing from headwaters in the mountains to their final destination in the ocean? I understood how rivers play an integral part of the water cycle. Streams and rivers form as runoff and precipitation collects and flows downhill toward the sea. Out of rivers grew seeds of the earliest civilizations. Cities develop where water provides all the resources to sustain life. But how would riding beside this waterway sustain *me*? What kinds of hardships would we encounter now, far from the places I have known?

Columbia River Gorge. The Columbia River spread wide and full, steely blue-gray light glinted off its smooth surface. Rolling alongside the water through this scenic terrain was easy. Trails here and there made for good photo rest stops. We found an old road that kept us off the well-traveled freeway. Signs and monuments were marked with legends and stories of the first settlers to pass through this country. Rather than worrying about the path ahead, I took an interest in the roadside markers—cultural and historical events cast in metal plaques, set in stones from the region. These stories explained how the waterways of the northwestern United States impacted migration, settlement, and the very survival of those who had come before. The waters of the Columbia, Snake, Deschutes, and Yellowstone play an essential role in the lives of humans, plants, animals—and bicyclists.

Journal Entry ~ July 14, 1974 A morning ride out of Portland, we're coming up on the Columbia River Gorge. Leaving behind hilly farms and ranches, we're dropping down toward the river bank. Between lacy fern dells and trees I spot steep walls of rock carved by waterfalls along the river's edge. I have to agree with Paul when he says there's something very soothing in the sounds of falling water. Following the course of the Columbia River is a natural choice as we head out of Portland on our eastward journey.

Once we turned away from the sea, we followed river courses toward the east. As long as we stayed by a river or stream we were assured the easiest path through and over mountains and geologic formations that would have otherwise been a barrier to our progress. Bicycling alongside these rivers helped smooth the way and boost our momentum. The waterways led us into the mountain passes, around peaks and eventually, in Wyoming, over the Continental Divide.

Mt. Hood National Forest borders on the Columbia, and we floated, like the water, through dripping forests that smelled of rain and green growing things. Picnic grounds and parks were many, right along the river's edge. Orchards and farms dotted the sloping hills, the scenery decorated with white water cascading over the sheer rock cliffs. Multnomah Falls, second in height only to Niagara, and Horsetail Falls, a waving watery sheet, poured over the cliffs into clear pools before blending with the Columbia.

We couldn't help but stop at every one of the waterfalls, and so the week passed pleasantly as we spent three nights camping along the path the Columbia had cut for us. One of these days we crossed over the Bridge of the Gods into Washington, simply to add one more state to our adventure. That was the best bridge! Riding across the steel structure on a metal mesh roadbed was a trip. Looking down past my feet strapped in the pedals I watched the waters flowing straight below me. Better than swimming, more fun than floating!

Legend of Klickitat and Wyeast. One afternoon we picnicked on the riverbank on the Washington side, and I pulled out a brochure I'd found at one of the parks. I convinced Paul to follow along with my storytelling as we tried to identify each of the peaks surrounding us.

"Let me tell you the Native American story about these volcanoes. See if you can find Mt. Hood, Mt. Adams, and Mt. St. Helens, all visible from near the Bridge of the Gods." Leaning against a tree, he closed his eyes to listen.

"Okay, according to the legend, there were different names for the two great Spirit Brother mountains. Mt Hood was called *Wyeast*, the Singer. It's the proud, pointy peak standing tall and confident, see it?"

"I see it. That's the closest one, just south of us. Kind of hidden from view with all the trees." he said. I was pleased how he was going along with my storytelling.

"Mt. Adams was *Klickitat*, the Totem Maker. He's bending his head down, I'll tell you why in a minute. The father, Warrior Multnomah, found this to be a beautiful place for his sons to settle. He shot one arrow to the south, and the other to the north of the river, marking spots where the mountains should live. Can you find Mt. Adams?"

"Yep, right up there almost opposite Mt. Hood."

"Multnomah created a stone bridge across the mighty Columbia, right here between the two mountains. Water flowed under a natural arch, the Bridge of the Gods, connecting the two brothers. Then, the beautiful Squaw Mountain moved into the valley between them. Naturally, the brothers both fell in love with her. They were angry, an argument erupted between the volcano brothers and they fought."

Paul looked like he was enjoying the shady rest, listening to the swooshing water lapping on shore. It seemed like he was paying attention.

"Go on, tell me. What happened then?"

"Klickitat and Wyeast spewed horrible smoke and fire, throwing around earth and stone, destroying the natural bridge. In the story, Klickitat won the battle and Squaw Mountain moved to his side, but because she really loved the other brother, Wyeast, she slumped over into a deep sleep. Does it look like Klickitat is bowing his head over her?"

"There's supposed to be a low mountain there beside Mt. Adams, where Squaw Mountain fell? I can't make it out. I guess we'll have to imagine it's there."

"One last part of the legend: When Wyeast and Klickitat were fighting, the guardian of the bridge, called *LooWit* (Mt. St. Helens), tried to protect the bridge. She wasn't able to stop the fight or keep the bridge from being destroyed. In her sadness she turned away and moved out of the main range of volcanoes. Where's Mt. St. Helens from here?'

"Looks like it may be that one way out to the west, not in a straight line from here. It's hard to tell which is which, so many snowy peaks."

He opened his arms and beckoned to me. "That's quite a romantic story considering they're a bunch of old volcanoes. Now, will you come over here and rest up a bit before we have to get going again?" I put my pen down, tucked in close to him by the tree, and leaned my head on his shoulder. It was delightful to connect ancient stories to our own adventures. We spent a peaceful afternoon resting in the shade, lulled by the sounds of the burbling river.

Race the Train. After our romantic volcano interlude by the shore, we got back on the bikes. Soon we were near Cascade Locks, where five massive diesel engines came whistling past on the tracks running right along the roadway, pulling a long freight train. I glanced at Paul, he grinned back, and together we flattened down to the drop bars, jammed on the pedals, and hauled into a race with the train. The engines roared in my ears. Boxcar wheels squealed and rattled along in a cacophony of power that rumbled through my bike frame. It was exhilarating riding as fast as possible for a couple of miles but, of course, the train just chugged on past and our only prize was a friendly wave from the man in the caboose watching us disappear as the train left us behind.

We crossed back to the Oregon side at Hood River and I called a friend I had worked with in California. She and her family had bought an old house to fix up. They were busy growing fruit, berries, chickens, and kids. Their five-acre place was covered in evergreen trees and they had plans to build a log cabin from the lumber on their property. We had a great home-cooked meal with them and they gave us a place to stay out of the rain overnight. In the morning we stuffed our panniers with Anne's homemade jam, cookies, and fresh pears that lasted us a few days. With a wave and a warning that in a few miles we would be suddenly in the Oregon desert, they sent us off and went back to work the land. Paul and I talked a bit about the contrasts—us traveling, them settled and carving out a life for their family. Someday, maybe, we'd grow a tree farm on the slopes of a volcano like Mt. Hood. That day, though, all we wanted was to see what we'd find around the next bend in the river.

Journal Entry ~ July 18, 1974 We're camped at Deschutes River Park. When we left The Dalles, the road was flat and wide. We made about 15 miles in less than 1.5 hours today, that's good time—fast, fun riding. We also left behind trees and cliffs and rock walls of the Columbia River Gorge. The Deschutes is wide and flowing fast. It is pleasant here, watching the water tumble along. Paul is taking advantage of the scenery and has been shooting lots of pictures of the beautiful sections we're riding through. Late start today but when the wind comes up in the afternoon it'll be blowing behind us and 40 miles isn't a difficult day's ride.

Finding Maps. Our method for navigating the route and planning daily ride goals was about to change. It had been relatively easy to follow the northbound coastal routes in California and Oregon and we tracked the course of the Columbia when we turned east. We'd traveled familiar territory, recognized city names, took the obvious roadways. From here on, in Eastern Oregon and beyond, we had to figure out where we wanted to go each day, how to get there, where to stop for camping and supplies.

We'd pick up regional, state, and local maps that were readily available in gas stations and convenience stores. We looked for detailed, clear maps that showed all the smaller roads, points of interest, and notes about campgrounds and services. Sometimes, the most helpful information was on a poster-sized map pasted on the door of a little store for travelers to find their way. But we liked carrying the paper maps with small red numbers printed alongside the routes between towns and landmarks. That was how we calculated our daily mileage and figured out how far we could go between stops. Paul had a pocket-sized notebook where he recorded each day's progress, did the math, and made our day-to-day plans. Those maps, often decorated with our notes and markings, were mailed back home periodically.

Making Miles. After the first month of riding, we had a good idea what our average speed was—10 or 12 miles per hour in normal conditions (mild weather, easy up-and-down hills). Our bodies told us when to stop. We could usually count on riding five or six hours before we'd need to rest, eat, and take some time off the bikes before settling in for the night. Up to this point, we averaged 40 to 50 miles each day. I wondered what kind of mileage we'd see in this new landscape.

The scenery changed abruptly at The Dalles. We came to a rise and pulled off to absorb the view, a broad ribbon of blue water winding through flat, empty desert. Who knew Oregon had desert? This would change things for sure, I thought. Until now, riding along the coast and through lush rainforests, we'd had no worries about water supply. In fact, the day before we had waded in the Columbia waters, just to cool our feet. But, as quickly as the north-south running Cascade Range was behind us, all the moisture from rainstorms blowing in from the coast halted their eastward run, blocked by the water-catching mountains. No storms, no rain, no sea breezes, just dirt. Brown earth lined the edges of the water flowing through the deep riverbed. No water runoff, no streams from here on—the land was barren. I was concerned.

Heat and Hills. I knew my legs were powerful and strong. My bike and I moved as one, balanced, smooth, and efficient. But here, something was sucking the energy out of me. In all the years spent playing and riding in California I had never sunburned, my skin tanned easily every summer. So why was I suddenly and completely depleted? The air was dry, the sun was hot, and I could not drink enough, fast enough, to replenish moisture and rehydrate.

"Paul, wait...!" I was shaking, sweating, and wilted in the stifling heat of the day.

"The hills are just too much. I just can't do it when it's this hot. If only there was a little breeze..." I pulled off the road and squished myself flat up against a hard rock cliff into a narrow slice of shade as the punishing midday sun beat down on the pavement. I was losing momentum. Paul agreed to find a spot for lunch, trying to comfort me.

"Hey, it's not so bad now. We made it up over the hill. And it didn't take so long, did it?" he said. "Look, have some food and rest up. You're just upset and it's making you feel tired."

"Yes, I am tired. And upset. And, well, this is NOT the last hill," I whined. "I just don't think..."

"Lynn, you want to do this trip, don't you? Are you afraid?"

"I am."

"Well, we won't melt—I'm sure of that. And today is not even so hot. We'll just take it slow and you'll see. Look how pretty this countryside is. Look around." Even while giving me encouraging words, he was obviously appreciating the wide open spaces.

It was just an attack of fear that quickly passed. I was extra tired because the night before, loud thunder and a wind storm had kept me awake. I'd been wakeful throughout the dark night watching the trees and power lines bend halfway to the ground in the gusts. I fully expected our tent to go any minute, too. Paul had, somehow, slept through it all and he was the strength that got us through that next day.

Finding My Focus. This part of the country challenged me with physical and emotional hardships and I struggled to make sense of it. I could find no sign of green, reassuring plant life around me. I craved beautiful blue waterscapes and greenery full of living things. Unfriendly, harsh landscapes were not welcoming so I searched inside for ways to comprehend this new land. No water to break up the earth, crackling golden brown scrub grasses barely poking through the dryness. I even scrubbed our cook pots with dirt on occasions where water was scarce.

I imagined after another few weeks of this arid, dusty riding I would understand the suffering of pioneers and could almost imagine what those ladies must have gone through. They had no real assurances that they would make it. I at least had my 12-ounce water bottle mounted on the down tube, so I sipped often and tried to keep my pace. I remembered to drink while we were stopped for meals and grabbed a few handfuls of dried fruit snacks as we pushed along, which helped replenish my energy. Paul continued to remind me that I was strong and that reminder was the force that drove me forward. Eventually, my body became acclimated and I felt comfortable on the bike once again.

Lewis & Clark. Seeing through the eyes of others who had inhabited these areas gave me a different focus. Hearing about the traditions, customs, and stories like the volcano legends gave me insight into how interpreting and living with nature could connect me with places I had never been. I took an interest in the first explorers to map a course through this part of the country and the pioneer families who later followed in their tracks. While riding the bike I tried to immerse myself in their stories and found a common thread that gave me a broader perspective.

We stopped at historical markers highlighting important events from the Lewis & Clark Expedition. More than 100 years before we passed this way, President Thomas Jefferson had commissioned naturalist Meriwether Lewis and official mapmaker William Clark to explore and chart the lands west of the Mississippi. The 33 members of this party used keelboats and canoes, sometimes hiking overland to survey unknown parts of the American West and establish the easiest route to the Pacific Ocean from Missouri. Lewis and Clark brought back invaluable information about Native peoples, their customs and languages, as well as collections of scientific and geological data. This marked the beginning of the westward expansion of the United States. Stopping at a bend in the river or next to a beautiful waterfall, we straddled our bikes and read the dates of the first sighting by these early explorers.

Much of their journey along the Columbia was by canoe, following the downriver course—the opposite direction from our trip. They were forced ashore by rapids and swirling waters where the width of the river was narrowed by rocky cliffs. Several dangerous boat rides over falls and rapids were documented in their logs. As we traveled along the same river on the bikes we passed a couple of dams and reservoirs with power plants that raised the water level and changed the flow of the river so there were no visible rapids. Human commerce had changed the character of the river and we pedaled along a quiet, serene Columbia.

Oregon Trail. Soon we found we were retracing the exact routes taken by the first white settlers to pass through this part of the country. Pioneers traveling between 1830 and 1870 followed trails essentially marked out by Lewis & Clark. They had come from the east in covered wagons, on horseback, and on foot. Stopping at every marker, I immersed myself in the stories of human struggle and discovery unfolding around us as we encountered the same views, the same natural wonders. At a fort in The Dalles we examined some of the original artifacts carried in wagon trains for 2,000 miles. They carried the essentials for starting a new life: copper pots, tea sets, skillets, silverware and soup ladles, quilts, bed frames, stools, farm tools and trunks to carry it all. We stopped at local libraries where I read through diaries and journals from Lewis and Clark as well as the earliest wagon train parties. I was curious: *What had changed since the migration 120 years before, what was still the same?*

Deschutes River Camp. We made camp on the shores of the Deschutes River whose waters flowed into the southern bank of the Columbia. In the still of the evening, after we were rested and full of dinner, we sat in shorts along the shore of this smaller, winding water course. It flowed faster than the wide Columbia and we read that many people didn't live through the crossing as they floated in prairie schooners across its rocky breadth. After all the hundreds of miles of suffering, within only a few days of their destination, some would drown. Some would watch belongings or family members be swept away by the current. In contrast, we had our bikes, our strength, and each other for support and a lot more knowledge of where we were going and what might lie ahead.

The serenity of the water and the peaceful light of sunset offered me a kinship with these riverways that I had not expected to find. Soon our road would take us away from the Columbia. A pattern began forming in my mind, that we were basically following water courses all the way across this land, just as the pioneers had done in their travels. Millions of years of steady water work had created the passes that would enable us to get across this mountainous country. In the old covered-wagon days, regular water sources were a necessity. For us, it meant more civilization as towns sprung up and thrived where consistent water was available.

A Long Day. One more day along the Columbia, after a loud thundering night that had kept me awake, a stormy tailwind blew us about 30 miles to the place where our road turned south and the river turned northward. Once again, I fought the sinking feeling—no water, no enthusiasm. The strong sunlight turned crispy scrub grass to a muted gold that held a fascination for Paul and awakened his photographic curiosity. I listened as he checked the map and ticked off the names of tiny towns out in the middle of nowhere:

"Wasco—20 miles, Cecil—14 miles, John Day—70 miles."

"Paul, if you're thinking of taking one of those roads off the main highway . . ."

"Well, yes, I am, sort of. That sure looks like a lot of pretty country and I'd like to see it. Look, it would be a shortcut, right through there we could cut off about 50 miles of riding to the Idaho border going at an angle like that."

"Nope, that's not the way I think we should go. Those are such small roads. There's nothing out there! If something happened we would be stranded in the middle of nowhere. No water and no place to stay or to get help. I don't want to follow you out there. I think it's safer on the highway."

Survival instincts, thirst, and lack of confidence momentarily drove me to envision a scenario where we'd split up because of my inability to keep up across the desolate Eastern Oregon countryside. But I had no alternative plan, so I remained stubborn.

It took a little convincing, but eventually he agreed we should stay together on the main road and we made our way on the longer, safer route toward the next state border. The storm winds stayed behind us and we sailed off along the flat, straight road, rolling fast. The heat was extreme and if we'd had any hills or wind resistance I would have been a lot worse off, but forward momentum created a little breeze to cool my skin. There was nothing to look at except the wide paved shoulder of pavement. We got a lot of attention that day from drivers tooting, waving, and yelling their approval. That gave us encouragement we needed and we kept going.

Late in the afternoon we both started to realize how hot it was getting and how long we'd been riding. We had to keep going, there was no place to stop even if we wanted to. Sooner than we imagined, we were nearing the town of Pendleton, Oregon.

Paul was still full of energy and couldn't hold back his enthusiasm. "Do you believe it? If we make it all the way to Pendleton we'll have made 70 miles today—actually, 72 miles!"

"Gosh! No, I really can't believe I made it this far. Even half a day in this desert sun seemed impossible. But, here we are!" I was beginning to realize I had more in me than I knew.

Journal Entry ~ July 19, 1974 Last night we got rained on, thundered at, and lightning-rattled in a summer storm. We had to move dinner inside to finish our Bisquik and jam. Paul tied the tent rope tight between a picnic table and the window of the men's room to protect us from wind, but gusts tried hard to blow the nylon roof off of us. I was wide awake much of the night while Paul slept through and clouds poured buckets. Wind was so steady that after a couple hours of storming, amazingly the tent was dry. This morning a glorious pink sunrise is warming the scene of the night's fury.

The Umatilla River formed a narrow canal and we coasted down a quick steep hill along the waterway into the next town. Civilization! I wanted ice cream! Forget empathizing with pioneers from the 1830s, I knew what I wanted and couldn't wait. A tiny grocery store freezer provided waffle cones and vanilla-chocolate swirls. The frozen treat was sweet, cold, and I let the drippings slide down my mouth and fingers. I could have stayed and eaten every cone from the freezer, but it was time to find a camp spot.

Pendleton had a rodeo grounds and campers would be welcomed in parks and backyards during the September rodeo roundup. But this was July and no one seemed ready to open a small space for our bikes and tent. Even the local police, although they were friendly, refused our request to stretch out on the shady front lawn of the city offices. We spoke to one sympathetic officer who lived up in the mountains and he offered to let us stay at his place, but it was 10 miles out of our way, uphill. Our two options seemed to be a trailer park somewhere out on the prairie or a state park about 30 miles out of town. How to explain, after you've spent 6 hours on a bicycle, riding over scorching pavement, that 30 more miles wasn't going to happen. To add to the challenge, a couple of people we spoke to asked if we knew about Cabbage Hill. They informed us, with a meaningful look and a laugh, we'd find out as soon as we got to the other side of town. A steep climb up part of the Blue Mountains—4300 feet elevation gain over 20 miles, at a 6-percent grade.

Bike Shop to the Rescue. With another problem to confront we did what we knew worked the best: hang around and talk about it for awhile, something would come up. This time, it was inside Bicycles to Go, a local bike shop just getting ready to close up for the day. By happy coincidence, it turned out the owner lived on the other side of Cabbage Hill, in La Grande. He offered to drive us over the hill to that state park and also suggested a little further on there was a rest area where we could camp for free.

He gave us and the bikes a ride 25 miles out of town, dropping us some 90 miles from our starting point that morning. We were in a beautiful little rest area maintained by the Oregon Highway system. The custodian came by to ask us about cleaning up after we left and he actually pointed out the smoothest piece of grass under some trees for us to pitch the tent. Turns out he'd been in charge of this rest area for a long time and loved bringing his grandchildren to play in "grandpa's park." We chatted for a bit and then, feeling numb from the day's ride, we fried up some spam and beans, fixed two cups of tea, and stretched out to rest. The sun set in a veil of heaven-pink clouds, the sky turned indigo velvet, and then a rainbow suddenly appeared across the top of the hill we were sitting on. Happiness welled up inside after such a day, surrounded by the beauty we had witnessed.

Anniversary Balloon. Mostly we sustained ourselves with canned conveniences and economic choices that would live well in the panniers for two or three days. Canned spam and beans, vegetables, stews, pastas, powdered soups, nuts and dried fruits or hard produce like apples, carrots, and fresh green beans were quick and easy. We supplemented those meals with the almost daily quart of milk and donuts when we could find them at break times, our best bet for extra mid-morning calories. On our five-month anniversary, July 16, we splurged with a box of salty-sweet Fiddle Faddle and celebrated with a blue helium balloon instead of donuts. The balloon bounced and floated, tied to my rear rack for the rest of the afternoon.

Gorging in La Grande. We needed to pick up groceries in La Grande, so we coasted quickly downhill after a slow start that morning. We spotted a market and the air conditioning felt so good we lingered a bit longer than necessary. Wandering around the shelves I came upon the case where they kept roast chickens and ribs and pork, steaming hot and all wrapped up, ready to go. Paul was stalling at the drinks section, turns out he had been craving a beer for a few days in all the heat. He came and found me and we took a look at a couple of rotisserie pork chops.

"How does that sound? Beer and pork chops for lunch? Well, why not, let's try it!"

The city park was the scene of our lunch gorge, with kids swimming and teens playing tennis. We shared the quart of Olympia and tore at juicy chunks of meat with our bare hands. It didn't take too long before we were both crashed out on our backs, happy under the dappled shade of some great oak trees. In an hour we awoke lazily and had a tough time grappling with the fact that we had more riding to do that day. How would we make it to the East Coast if we spent many afternoons lollygagging like this!

Further down the road, we had possibly our most memorable cooking experience. The town of North Powder was ahead of us, but we found the main street had closed for the night. Surprisingly, many hamlets like this consisted of one guy who ran the gas station and one other one who owned the store where the post office was housed around the aisle between the milk and bread. It was just past 6 p.m., still light and warm, but terribly windy. I was ready to stop, anywhere, get something to eat, and take a break.

We came upon a section of road under construction. On that Saturday night all the trucks and tractors had been parked and deserted for the weekend. We pulled up alongside a huge yellow Hyster steam roller positioned in the middle of a strip of newly hardened concrete roadbed. Paul investigated, assessed the wind, and gave his approval. I confidently set up our one-burner stove on the steel step leading up to the seat in the open cab. We enjoyed our canned tamales and beans in the shade and out of the wind, the perfect level spot for a feast. That night I was convinced for sure that I would never settle again into a kitchen cooking regular food with everyday household appliances.

The next day was Sunday, and we found ourselves in Durkee, a tiny town outside Ontario. A couple of cowboys hopped out of their truck in front of the General Store and asked us where we were from. We'd traveled a long way and were far from touristed areas, so more and more people stopped to chat with us. In camp or rest areas, people strolled by and asked about our trip and they would be amazed. But each time we turned the question around we heard about how important *their* trip was. A young woman was headed to Spokane for a family gathering; a couple going to visit Canada for the first time because they'd never been up that far. A man and his daughter enjoying a summer vacation together. Everyone's story was exciting to them, and I continued to be fascinated by how many interesting and different folks we connected with—all travelers on our journeys, all exploring this world in our own unique way.

Farewell Bend. Our last day in Oregon was undoubtedly the worst. Temperatures were the hottest we'd had so far, and only one town popped up over the 50 miles we rode before we stopped for the night at Huntington. This spot near the state border had once been a switching station for Union Pacific Railroad crews, but recent changes had occurred so only two or three freights came through each day. Families were moving out and the population had suddenly dropped to about 350 residents. The town was clearly depressed.

We climbed off the bikes and walked up a small hill to investigate the cemetery a couple of miles beyond the town. Sun had been beating down for more than a century on these mounds, cracking the scorched surface. Prickly weeds spread across the hillside and every one of the gravestones leaned to one side or another. Most of the inscriptions showed dates in the 1870s but we found a few more marked with recent dates. Rusted coffee cans held the remnants of plastic flowers and under one desert sage brush we found a wooden slate with the name Richard Greenscade. The top of the marker was charred, perhaps from a long-ago fire. We sat there among the graves, looking down at the cluster of trees and roofs of Huntington, dying in its own way because of the disappearing railroad.

We turned toward the southeast and saw Farewell Bend campground below us, tucked alongside the winding Snake River. This was where wagon trains stopped for their last water on the eastward trail they had followed for 300 miles. From here, we knew from having just bicycled through, they would meet the desolate, harsh, and unknown territory of Eastern Oregon. We went a little out of our way so we could picnic on the banks of the Snake at the campground. Then, back on the bikes to get to the Idaho border.

We faced a long, steep grade. It didn't look exactly like hills I'd seen because there were no landmarks or points of reference to gauge the distance. Only the empty, hot road ahead, laid out on a continuous uphill slant. It was always scary for me to start at a steep angle like that and not be able to see how far it would be to the top. The wind was slight and blowing just the same speed and direction we were traveling so there was no airflow to provide cooling as I sweated up the hill. I stopped and complained quite a few times and sipped at the water bottle every few minutes, letting the cooling drops linger on the tip of my tongue, hoping it wouldn't evaporate too quickly.

It took us about a half hour and probably three miles of steady climbing before we could see the top. I struggled, pushed, and forced my legs to go around until finally the hill flattened at a curve in the road. Then, as we rounded the curve and I could almost catch a deep breath again, I glanced across the landscape only to find—another hill! There was the hard-earned downhill coast, of equal length and angle to match the uphill we had gained. But across the low spot was an identical, long steep climb up to the same level. From a wide enough vantage point I'm sure it would have looked like a roller coaster track, but I was feeling anything but amused. It was hot and difficult and there was nothing to be done but keep on pushing. So, freefall coast for another mile and then a long, slow slog to the crest of the second hill of the day. We could see Ontario below where there would be mail for us at General Delivery. That gave me motivation to keep on going.

Trucker on the Hill. A double-trailer semi-truck tooted at us and pulled off as we paused at the crest of that second hill. We had been seeing trucks every day and wondered how truckers passed their time, back and forth along the same roads day in and day out. Often the only other humans we'd see for hours, we happily waved to them and mostly they waved back.

"Wonder what he wants? Maybe just stopping for lunch?" Paul suggested.

"Hello, How ya doin?" called the driver through his window. "They sure grow big hills out here, don't they?" He seemed jovial, so we nodded a hello back.

"You guys traveling far? I think I saw you a few days ago on this road on my way north. You must be quite a ways from home."

We told him a little about our trip, where we'd started and our destination ahead. We asked him about where he lived, did he like being on the road all the time? He explained his family lived in Salt Lake City. Then we were surprised to learn he lived mostly between there and Washington, inside his truck. He offered to give us a ride for as long as we wanted. He'd have taken us all the way to Salt Lake if we were headed there, or to Ontario, which was now in sight and, naturally, all downhill from where we were chatting.

At that point, Paul explained, there was no need for a ride, we'd prefer to stay on the bikes, and I was ready for a well-earned downhill spell. He showed us his map and made suggestions for some less hilly routes. I got the impression he would have liked our company and to have someone to talk to for the rest of the day. We thanked him and headed off with a wave and a smile, thinking of the unique lifestyle of long-distance truckers and how that compared to our own long-distance trip.

On the way down the giant hill, we stopped again by the side of the road so Paul could get a good photo of the rolling hills, the river, and the mountainous terrain off in the distance. He took his camera out into the weeds to frame some shots, so I left him concentrating on capturing the light and the view while I drank more from my half-empty water bottle. He came back with a tiny flower to cheer me—a dried, baked starburst remnant of a bloom radiating points from its spent seed head. It was a sweet gesture and he tucked the little flower branch into the blue bandana that held my hair back.

The wide-open spaces so inspired him—and I was missing the ocean.

Idaho Border. Very quickly we were over the border into Idaho and on the course of the Snake River. The Snake became my companion the same as the Columbia had been, as this smaller stream flowed right into the Columbia on its way to the sea. Right away I noticed the effects of irrigation that transformed the unfriendly dust into farmlands. The broad reaches of the Snake and its many tributaries opened up many miles of green vistas to enjoy. The interstate we had been following suddenly prohibited bikers and so we adjusted our course a little and took rural farm roads through tiny towns. The air was different, scented with moisture, and I knew we were no longer in the desert. It was still pretty hot and very humid. I was greeted by the smell of the most effective fertilizer on rural farms: manure.

We headed for the capital, Boise, for the night, but were not anxious to spend time riding in the city. We asked around and were directed to a commercial campground on the other side of town. It was expensive and crowded with families unfolding circus-like tents decorated with fringe and mosquito netting. We sat and watched while groups of campers commandeered two or three picnic tables and gathered around generators or battery-operated televisions to watch their favorite programs and snack on watermelon and s'mores. A hoard of little boys trailed behind a man with a metal detector, digging up every spot where the machine ticked a signal.

As we tried to settle in and arrange our tent after dinner, a middle-aged man stopped by. He was riding a popsicle yellow 10-speed.

"Hi, how are you?"

"Hello. Doing fine, how about you?" Paul answered.

"Maybe you two can tell me what it's really like on a bicycle tour," he explained. "I'm planning to take a bunch of kids on a bike trip through Yellowstone Park down to Jackson Hole. We're leaving in a couple of weeks and it will be a 150-mile trip. Right now I'm just hoping I'll be in shape for it."

"Oh, you will be, after the first day," Paul said, smiling knowingly.

He asked a lot of questions about our trip and bicycle touring. An interesting fellow, he said he was a traveling salesman and he shared some philosophical thoughts as we sat and visited. We listened to his stories until it got late and we said good night. As it turned out, we were destined to meet him again soon.

The next day we knew we would face a 50-mile stretch of inhospitable highway riding, so we stalled around until noontime and had lunch in an old roadside truck stop that looked like it was on its last leg. Inside, the diner sported wooden booths, an old horseshoe-shaped counter surrounded by vinyl upholstered stools and decorated with plastic plants. We were the only ones there and the waitress didn't seem to be in a mood for conversation, so we ate quietly, returned the empty glass Coke bottles for our ten-cent deposit, and left.

Then, to perk up our day, a series of humorous advertising signs appeared along the road just past the truck stop:

"Sage brush is free—Stuff some in your car."

"Idaho skunks are not to be sniffed at."

"Petrified Watermelons—take some home to your mother-in-law."

As we continued on, the winds kept me moving at a slow pace, following varied topography formed by the course of the river. In places the land was lush and irrigated, with springs gushing through volcanic rock. Other spots revealed deep narrow chasms where the water had eroded and carved a path through hard granite-like stone. The hills had been difficult, but the river was a gentle guide, easing my way forward.

The heat had made for some sluggish riding and this time we were both feeling a lack of energy. We were on a stretch of deserted road paralleling the highway, hoping to catch a more northerly route that might make the riding easier. For a couple of days we had not been altogether sure of the highway system, trying to find roads that were legal for bicycles, which ones would be paved all the way and which ones actually were through roads leading to someplace. We didn't know exactly where we were or where we wanted to go and how we would get there. Our plan was to ride along the empty stretch of road, aiming for two little black marks on the map that may or may not indicate a rest area. We headed for the junction hoping we would find water and a place to camp.

Flat Tires and Lost Tools. POW... hissssss ... that was a familiar sound. Flat tires seemed to follow Paul around in spells. He had already popped three or four tubes since the start, and we were on the lookout for some replacement spare tubes. His rear tire limped flatly along the road, it was getting late and we had not seen a car or signs of life for a couple of hours. A flat wasn't normally that big of a hassle, but when it was the back wheel it meant all the equipment had to come off the bike: panniers, sleeping bag, straps, and the derailleur and chain. This was the fifth flat he'd had and then, unbelievably, we discovered both tire pumps we carried were broken. He was able to squeeze just about enough air into the tube to let us limp slowly over the rough road, not knowing for sure what was ahead.

We made it just to the rest area and, when Paul dismounted to walk the bike across the divider, the tire blew again—this time we saw the thorn sticking out and had something obvious to curse. At the end of a day's ride it was just too awful to think of repairing a tire, so we decided to chill for the night and face things in the morning.

We were at a truck weigh station along Highway 80N, in the desert wasteland that was southern Idaho—we had reached the black marks on the map we had been looking for. We scoped out a small building, wide asphalt drives on either side, a restroom, and a few picnic tables on some grass punctuated with a couple of pathetic little trees. We asked the guy in the station if we could camp and he snickered.

"Sure, anywhere you like. The trucks come in all day and all night. Might be noisy. Oh, and the sprinkler system comes on automatically at 4 a.m. But you can pick any spot you want."

Not in a good mood to start with, this was not our best choice, but it was what we had.

"The mosquitoes aren't bad here, at least," Paul ventured.

"Okay, yeah. I don't think those cows in the field over there are going to bother us, either," I quipped.

"Which patch of grass looks the driest? Maybe over there? We've been rained on before, it'll be okay."

With zero enthusiasm, we pitched the tent and settled down. By 7:30 we were inside the tent with a warm pot of beans—the spotlight from the parking lot lighting up our dinner plates and shining brightly on the sleeping bags.

Peaceful as babes, we slept through probably 20 or 30 truckers pulling in to get weighed, share some gossip, and have a midnight picnic. The incessant roar of engine sounds wasn't quite steady enough to allow for a deep sleep. At some point in the middle of the night, a radio blared us fully awake with a rousing chorus of Johnny Horton's "Battle of New Orleans!" Not able to sleep, but still totally exhausted, we could not help but laugh out loud.

Of course, right on schedule, the sprinklers turned on at 4:00. Felt like rain, no, it must be hail! Paul didn't even take his socks off. He jumped out of the tent and jammed a rock into the offending rotating sprinkler so it sprayed a 40-foot arc away from our tent and out into the parking lot. Nothing to do then but wait till dawn and fix that flat.

The next day the air hose at the truck stop gave Paul's patched tube a new lease on life. Low on energy, we progressed a whopping 26 miles. After that unforgettable night at the weigh station, everything we encountered seemed disproportionately hilarious. After so many weeks of travel, having shared so many unique experiences, we were somehow feeling set apart—no one but us had been through what we had.

We camped at another historic spot on the Oregon Trail, a town park at Register Rock. A family picnicking near us noticed our bikes. The dad came over to find out what we were up to.

"Hi, we just wanted to find out where you two are from. Where are you headed?"

"Hi. We came from California, and we're biking to the east coast, where are you from?" I asked.

He mentioned Pocatello, not too far down the road. We got him talking about their Sunday picnic and then he asked us, "Would you like some watermelon?" We only hesitated for a second. He brought us a whole melon, cut into chunks. We never asked his name, we probably didn't adequately thank him for such a treat as cold watermelon in summer on the road in the heat. The family watched from across the park as we wolfed down the melon and it looked like they were pleased with our reaction as we smiled through watermelon juice dripping down our chins.

The land changed dramatically as we found ourselves on the east side of the Snake River. One side was bordered with rocks and sharp jagged black lava cliffs; the other side opened into a fertile valley full of farms and desert-like hills in the distance. We dropped down into the valley and watched a hay baling machine at work along the road, harvesting the wide farm covered in acres of grain.

After 30 miles of riding we settled on a grassy rest area with some shade trees to camp for the night. We sat for awhile, resting at a picnic table before setting up the tent, and noticed a truck pulled up. The man who got out was the same one we had met and chatted with a couple of days earlier riding the bright yellow 10-speed. He came over and recognized us, shook our hands with a cheerful greeting. This time he told us he was a candy distributor for the company who made 5th

Avenue and Peanut Butter bars. He was just as full of life and stories to tell, but this time he was working and eager to get on with his trip. Before he left, he pulled out four bags of candy samples from his case and gave them to us. We eagerly accepted the gift and began nibbling through the heap of surprise treats.

Journal Entry ~ July 25, 1974 After supper, in the cool and quiet evening, Paul and I talked for awhile about future plans and what we might like to accomplish. He is seeing how our goals have changed—and become more solidified—since we've been traveling together. And I am noticing how our communication style is different. More intense, and sometimes harsh on the days we feel stressed and tired, but our talks are always caring and meaningful. We're definitely more together now, more in sync, than we would have ever been. An image of a big house with a wraparound porch, full of warmth and family, is becoming more vivid. Then, packing up our stuff before we crawled into the tent we realized the denim bag of tools is gone. Wrench, pliers, screwdriver, tire irons. Don't know where or how, but it disappeared within the last two days. We'll need to pick up some bike repair essentials as soon as we can. In the meantime, it seems we're also gathering tools we can use to build our life together while we figure out how to meet the challenges ahead.

General Delivery. Our next stop was American Falls, Idaho, at the post office.

"Hartman? Oh yes, do we have something for you!" the postman spoke to us like we were old friends. Then from the General Delivery shelf he pulled down a big package, half a dozen letters, and a couple of manila envelopes all with our name on them. We recognized handwriting from both coasts—Paul's family in New York and mine in

Santa Barbara. We were thrilled to hear from home and pretty stoked to get those packages opened. We gathered everything up and stepped out the door, spreading it all out on the sidewalk right in front of the post office. We knifed the box open, dug in, and started pulling out goodies.

There were letters from almost everyone, brothers and sisters and parents. Paul pulled out some film and there were extra film cans stuffed with surprise candies and treats. I unwrapped a cucumber, home grown in my dad's garden, two California avocados, some cash from Paul's sister in Delaware, and two aluminum coffee cans full of homemade chocolate chip cookies. Oblivious to what we might have looked like, we were surprised by a woman who let us know about the park down the road if we maybe wanted to have a picnic. So, we picked up our treasures, cookies and all, and headed over to the park.

Airstream Friends. We set up some of our equipment on a picnic table and polished off half a can of cookies before thinking of lunch. We started writing letters home and then someone else surprised us. An older, balding man appeared next to the table.

"Pardon me, but my wife and I were wondering if you two are really traveling on those things," he pointed to the bikes leaning in the shade.

"That's right, we are," Paul answered.

"How far ya goin'?"

"Well, we started in California, at her parents' house. We're headed for New York, where my parents live."

"Is that right?" He was looking back and forth from me to Paul. "How many miles can you make on them, anyway, in a day?"

"About 50 a day, when the weather's right," Paul told him.

"Now, tell me, what's it like ridin' like that? It just doesn't seem possible you could do that," he said. His wife was coming over now, white-haired, and full of smiles. She stood by her husband, a tall, agile man who we guessed was in his 60s.

"We travel around in our travel-trailer for 9 or 10 months out of the year," she said. "We have a house in Birmingham, Alabama. All our kids are grown now, we only go home for Christmas, really."

Her husband remarked, "Some of the best fishin' in the country is right here in Idaho. We follow the fish around, come back here usually every year to this park for a couple of weeks. See the same folks every year and find out about people we'd met in other camp places."

He introduced himself as Albert Jones and his wife, Odell. They excused themselves and said they'd let us go and enjoy our picnic. Then, in a few minutes Albert came back to ask one more question about the bikes. "Say have you folks had lunch? Come on over to the trailer, Odell will fix us up some sandwiches. Come on, we like talking to people." So, we followed.

Odell invited me into the airstream to fix up bologna sandwiches the way Paul liked them—but I realized I wasn't sure yet what he liked on his sandwiches, we hadn't been married that long. She led me into their modest home on wheels, poured a bucket of water for me to wash my hands, and told me about their traveling life. Albert fished, mostly, and she liked to stay in camp and talk with the other wives, watch tv, just relax in the parks. The year before, on one of their trips, their trailer had rolled over and wrecked. They flew home, went right out and bought themselves a new one just like the old one, and started the trip again. She handed me crisp leaves of fresh lettuce for the sandwiches as she explained that they planned to keep traveling every summer.

Sharing Stories. Outside, Paul was hearing about how Albert had hoboed as a young boy, some 40 years ago. He hitched rides on trains with a friend all the way to Texas. They worked awhile at a farm, bought two balloon-tired bikes, and set out with bedrolls and food to ride their bikes home to Alabama. The second day out they hit a big rocky section of the unpaved road, collided head on and totaled both bikes. They had to hobo all the way back. His eyes were sparkling and I could tell that he was still wishing he could travel the world.

Odell and I joined them with the sandwiches and chips on a tray as Paul spoke next. "We just met a guy the other day, about 70 years old, wiry and leather-skinned, riding a bicycle in Buhl, Idaho. He said he rides about 12,000 miles every year, through Montana, Oregon, Idaho, and down to Southern California. He was doing great. You could do it, too, you know," Paul smiled.

"Well, say, did that old man have a pretty little white-haired lady along with him? Cause if I was to go, I'd have to take Odell. When I was sick the other day she was so good to me. I couldn't ever leave her behind. She's a positive jewel," he laughed out loud.

The Joneses told us the most important, exciting part of life was the people they met. In their travels they had made friends, helped strangers, and been helped by many others.

"Most everybody you meet are good folks, given a chance. Most everyone. The majority of people in the world are good, and it's not what you hear about, but it's the truth," Albert said. They were full of tales to tell us and quietly interested in hearing ours, so we spent the whole afternoon there in the park, with not a thought to the miles ahead. Taking time with people we met on the road was always rich and rewarding. The rest of that afternoon put me in such a great mood, full of news from home and cookies, and the good vibe from being with friendly people. We traveled through farmlands and tiny towns and found a camp in a little fishing community. Once again comfortably cruising along the shores of the Snake River, we were blissfully unaware of how soon the scenery would change.

6  MOUNTAINS

Idaho . Wyoming

Cyclists can usually find drama around any kind of mountainous country. A hill often provides an interesting challenge, but a mountain range might well be a barrier—the force of gravity pulling against upward momentum, hindering forward progress. By that same principle, what goes up must come down. We faced these forces head on, mounted on our two-wheeled steeds, and surprised ourselves several times from the moment we left the gently flowing Snake and encountered our first significant elevation gains. The atmosphere above mountain passes and across high plateaus was rarified and thin. My lungs gasped for oxygen, but the clarity and pure unpolluted sweetness of the air was uplifting and invigorating.

Idaho to Wyoming. A storm was brewing as we headed toward the pass that everyone told us was the wrong way to go. We ignored the historic wisdom of the pioneers and instead of following the Snake River around the mountains at the Idaho border we chose the more scenic, more mountainous route that would take us over Pine Creek Pass: elevation 6720 feet.

Following the gradual rising road out of the Snake River plain, we climbed in steady, step-like progression up a series of plateaus—one or two hundred feet at a time over a total distance of 40 or 50 miles. As the river sliced a rift canyon into the mountains, we were above 5,000 feet and it seemed like we had gained a slight head start before leaving the course of the Snake. We soon found ourselves following the narrow trickle of Pine Creek, a mountain stream that led the way into the Teton Range.

Out of the broad plateau lands we passed fields of fading green and golden grain. I spotted an old abandoned log farmhouse given over to wild vines that crawled over the walls and windows and into the doorway. Paul was captivated by the scene so we stopped briefly for some pictures and to enjoy the pastoral view. After the short interlude we mounted up and, just around a little bend, suddenly a thick pine and fir forest encompassed us. A gracefully arched concrete bridge took us high over the path of Pine Creek as it meandered through the trees and foothills. When the road descended to the banks, we stopped to fill our water bottles from the cool, clear stream where it tumbled over colorful stones flashing blues, pinks, and grays through the sunlit ripples.

The rain finally overtook us and once again we fell into an unexpected surprise. Out of Swan Valley, a wide green pastureland, we could see squalls building and rain spilling from the sky all around us. I was not anxious to get caught in any kind of downpour that day.

"Paul, let's stop for lunch here, okay?" I yelled ahead.

Paul was skeptical. "Really, you're thinking we can find someplace to stop on this road?"

"I'll keep an eye out. I really don't want to ride into one of those patches of freezing cold water!"

After some deliberation, we came upon the one-street town of Victor, found a small grassy park, and started unpacking our gear to make a nice lunch. Just as I had everything spread out on the table, a sudden loud crack of thunder broke from above, followed by a powerful gust of wind that blew our plates, pots, utensils, food packages, and lemonade off the table and clear across the park. We ran around the lawn, gathered everything into armloads, and headed for the shelter of a nearby building that turned out to be the Valley of the Tetons Library. We tried to settle down again to get some lunch ready, but the crazy wind made it impossible.

No one but a couple of bicyclists a couple thousand miles from home would think to ask, but Paul ducked in through the entrance to see if the librarian would let us eat inside. He came out grinning. He had caught the librarian napping on the couch and so what could she say but, sure, we could come in and use the landing of the basement stairs for our picnic. We enjoyed a calm, quiet lunch and then treated ourselves to some reading—the history of the Teton Valley and a little of Mark Twain's humor—while we escaped the downpour outside. The library closed early that day, so we had to leave our happy sanctuary. In a few miles we found an out-of-the-way forest service camp at the base of the giant mountain pass we'd face the next day. It was our last day in Idaho.

Journal Entry ~ August 1, 1974 **(2000 miles)** *Paul's having a nap now. A little stream ripples behind me and we're near enough to sense there are mountains looming ahead. I'm feeling some anxiety, but also a little excitement thinking of how it will feel to be on the other side of this mountain pass. We're coming up on our second thousand miles after less than two months of traveling. Our habits have evolved as we've camped, shopped, cooked, ridden. A lot of it is routine now—just us, rolling down the road. Our focus isn't so much on miles per day or concerns over where we camp or when it'll be suppertime. We notice more the little things around us and what we're learning, like the ways small towns attract us—or often distract us—from our eastward goal. We wonder more about the people we meet, community, nature, geological influences, and local history. Then, the circle closes because as we learn about others we become more familiar with ourselves and develop a deeper understanding of each other. Because of our openness to new, shared experiences, Paul and I have grown closer. We're establishing our way of life, mapping out a direction that will shape our dreams. If and when we stop for a life that's more permanent than bike touring, I can imagine our dreams becoming reality.*

Teton Pass. We awoke early the next morning, feeling strong and ready to tackle Teton Pass. Starting at around 6,000 feet, we prepared to climb the 8,400-foot summit. This was our first true mountain pass and neither of us knew what was in store. *How did we ever think we were going to get up that mountain?* Even in first gear it seemed impossible, impassible. We fought the laws of gravity, ignoring the fact that our bodies might have had limits of physical strength. The crisp mountain air, majestic pines, and deep earth scents rising from forest undergrowth gave us confidence as we tackled the uphill climb, watching the early morning sunbeams splash across the peaks.

I pushed hard on the cranks. One foot down. Another foot down. Stroke down with one leg, pull up with the other. The 27-inch wheels kept revolving, taking me forward, a few feet at a time. We took turns begging to stop at regular five-minute intervals. I'd pull over to the shoulder and rest for a couple of minutes, letting my breath catch up with the climbing as my lungs adjusted to the elevation gain. Then, Paul would run out of breath and he needed to stop. I waited for him. He waited for me. Eventually it became simply too steep to get the pack-laden bikes moving again if we stopped. Traffic was nonexistent that early in the morning so we stayed right in the middle of the road, tracing switchbacks as we struggled on. Somewhere along that road I knew we'd crossed into Wyoming, but I was too preoccupied to notice the border sign. The steep angle of pavement leading into blind curves on the mountainside gave no clue how far it would be to the top. I pumped my thigh muscles hard—contracting, then releasing—keeping momentum for more than two hours up the slope.

At last—the summit came into view. I slowed while Paul stopped for a photo. Lungs straining to replenish the oxygen, heart pounding from the effort, I couldn't hold back a smile as I gazed across the expanse of landscape. Alpine meadows, shrubs and grasses waved across a carpet of bright morning colors, a soft breeze. We'd made it to the top, the wooden sign confirmed it: 8431 Feet Elevation! A sensation of weightlessness—part of me swelled with pride at the accomplishment, part of me gasped in awe and thanksgiving for legs and determination enough to get me up such a challenging climb and grant me an incredible view. Below sat Jackson Hole, Wyoming, and our old friend the Snake River once again looping around on its steady course westward.

And then...the downhill ride. Wind battered the skin on my face and arms. I gripped the handlebars tight but boldly let loose on the hand brakes. Tears of joy streaked down my cheeks. Cars chugging up the steep other side almost drove off the edge as drivers and passengers stared at us blazing by. A construction sign at the top showed it was 5 miles to the bottom and Paul clocked us by his wristwatch at 7 minutes for the sweet thrill of a five-mile-long glide. Forty miles an hour on a bike!

Jackson Hole. The historic town of Jackson Hole nestled in a deep, flat valley between towering mountains. It was once a central location for fur trading, first settled by John Colter who, as it turned out, was a member of the Lewis and Clark expedition. The town retained the character of the Old West with wooden sidewalks, an ornate balcony over the saloon, and a huge arch of tangled elk horns gracing the entrance to the central park. It was mildly entertaining, but I found I had developed my taste of the western flavor bicycling every mile of this distinctive section of the country. The West to me lived as a vast expanse of dramatic landforms, individuals eking out their living in unforgiving surroundings. My sentiments toward this excess were echoed by a little girl holding onto her father's hand, when she complained, "There's nothing but cowboy stuff around here!"

Tourists flocked to Jackson on their way to Grand Tetons and Yellowstone National Park. We found the hustle and bustle of even this small town a bit too intense after our climb. We stayed only long enough to tell whoever would listen about our amazing downhill experience. We enjoyed a couple of well-earned juicy, salty hamburgers and piles of fries, and then headed north to ride through the National Elk Reserve on the way to the Tetons. I hoped to see the elk herds, but also hoped we wouldn't see them up close.

The Tetons displayed a magnificent, astonishing view as I gazed up at a wall of granite rock and earth jutting 13,766 feet into the sky. Three jagged crags stood like a row of warriors reaching up to challenge the clouds. Native Americans called them the Great White-Headed Fathers, while French fur trappers in the early 1800s gave them the name Les Troix Tetons—the three breasts. I learned that the sharp, rough peaks indicated a young range, time and erosion had not yet made its mark by rounding and smoothing some of the oldest rocks in North America. According to the National Park brochure, similar forces that formed the Himalayas also caused the Teton Range to rise when tectonic plates collided. Me and my bike appeared as an insignificant green dot crawling alongside the immense peaks.

Yet, as always, practical realities snapped us back from the scenery and reminded us to deal with our immediate needs. We were tired and all the campgrounds were filled to capacity. We began asking at Moose Junction campground and checked with other spots ahead. Rangers were friendly but were not able to bend the rules for two weary bikers—they were used to managing a million visitors a month and needed to maintain strict policies. Our only alternative was to ride back about 10 miles where there were still some openings and hope, hope, hope we would find a space when we got there. Since we were in national park lands, we were not allowed to simply pull off the road to find spots to camp out, and we heard that all through Yellowstone campgrounds were filling by 3 p.m. We were in trouble.

"So, what do you want to do?" Paul asked me.

"Oh, man, with this information about how quickly the campsites fill up, we need some kind of plan. All the tourists in cars will for sure get to every camp spot way before we could, riding our bikes between available campgrounds!"

I was thinking of our possibilities. Considering all the good fortune we'd had, our positive attitude that everything would always work out, that day I did not have the confidence to just wait and see what would happen. We faced the overwhelming presence of summer crowds converging on a popular national park. This time, we needed to take some action.

"It's too late for today. Looks like we need to backtrack to that place they say isn't full yet. I guess maybe we ought to call ahead and reserve spaces when we expect to be at the sites further on in Yellowstone. What do you think?"

Paul pulled out the map we had picked up at the entrance to check distances between camps.

"I think we can figure on at least three nights in the park. Hang on and I'll check the mileage we could make each day and find out where the camps are."

"Okay, good, then I'll call from the phone booth at that camp we passed back there."

I would feel better if we were sure where we could set up camp, hopefully where we would not be exposed to the animals roaming free in the wilds. Paul read out the names of the campgrounds: Grant Village, Norris Basin, Fishing Bridge, and for one night we could afford to rent a rustic cabin near the lodge. I was able to secure four nights' reservations in Yellowstone. However, that did not solve the issue of our next two nights before we got into the next national park.

Not certain where we would sleep that night, we retraced back the 10 miles toward the camp that momentarily had sites—hoping we'd beat the campers riding in cars. We became totally distracted by the changing moods of light and shadow cast by clouds over the face of the Grand Tetons. Crystal clear lakes at the base of the three peaks reflected rock and ice off the mountaintops. Glacial moraine mounds spread at their feet, forming a wide valley dotted with Lodgepole pines and prairie grasses. At one particularly gorgeous view spot, we spoke with an artist from Indiana. We watched him awhile as he filled his canvas with shades of gray and blue to capture the splendor of the peaks against the sky. Every summer, he explained, he traveled with his easel and oils, sketching and painting. Back in his studio he would complete his pictures to sell, supporting his family from the summer's fruits of adventure.

Sharing Camp. We beat the odds and secured a campsite. Several hikers and climbers were gathered at the ranger hut preparing for a trek through the wilderness and up the sides of those mountains. We recognized camaraderie in these fellow travelers, so we invited a couple from North Carolina to share our prized campsite. It was interesting comparing notes of our journeys and what we were each looking forward to seeing, different modes of travel as well as different goals. I wasn't sure if I would be brave enough to attempt a climb even part way up the 13,000-foot sheer rock face. Experienced rangers and guides were there to answer questions, help plan routes, and provide details about the trails before hikers set out. I was definitely happier and more confident sticking with my two wheels on flatter ground.

The next afternoon, as we pulled into what we expected would be another full campground in the Tetons, we stood at the ranger shack, waiting to hear that there were no spaces left. We had pushed all day as fast as we could, but it looked like we hadn't made it in time to snag a campsite.

"Hi, you guys riding bikes through the parks here?"

A fellow about our age walked up to us from inside the campground. He sported shoulder-length dark hair, a shaggy moustache, and an even bigger friendly grin.

"Yeah, we've ridden all the way from California and now we find out we can't even stay here for the night! You know of any empty spots to camp?" I asked, hopefully.

"Well, hey, cool! I'm from Berkeley. Have my bike in the truck. Say, if you don't find a place, this is my campsite number. I'm already on the ranger's demerit list, so come and share with me. The place next to me is empty right now, and there's room for about 12 people where I'm set up." He handed us a scrap of paper and gave us directions to find his vehicle before he headed off to explore.

Our turn came to check with the ranger—no luck, no unreserved spaces available. He even mentioned it's against the rules to double up in campsites, apparently having heard our discussion with the guy from Berkeley. Well, we were on bikes, not driving a car, it was starting to rain and we were just tired enough to risk getting into trouble. We found our way to Rob Mearing's camp and decided we would be camp-mates for the next few days.

The natural resources/geography/political science graduate student from Berkeley became our companion and good friend as we shared a picnic table and settled our bikes near his truck. He was on summer break—exploring, traveling, and looking for someone to share expenses with. We arranged to meet at all the camp spots in Yellowstone that Paul and I had made. He was happy to have a place on those nights. We swapped stories over a campfire, a pleasant departure from our established routine for getting through quick suppers and early bedtimes. I was curious about his experiences in the counterculture movement at UC Berkeley. He and Paul compared notes about their very different navy lives: Paul on a carrier ship and Rob as a supply officer. He explained he had missed the 1969 People's Park riots, he seemed actually to be more of a free-thinking individual, kind of like us, just doing his own thing.

Camping with Moose. Rob carried supplies to make fresh-brewed coffee. He was lively, full of fun, and full of jokes. We made a connection and he had questions about our bicycling experience. The evening was a treat since we all had a collection of adventures to share. We totally enjoyed staying up late listening to the tales he told.

Later that night, a moose came by to visit the nearby camps. An enormous moose! Not quite an elephant, but for sure the largest wild thing I'd ever encountered. Massive antlers as wide as a billboard spread side to side above a snout that seemed big enough to devour the front half of a VW Bug. Paul took his 35mm lens and stayed a good distance back from the dangerous-looking beast to try to get a photo. A woman from Ohio just walked up to the animal, coaxing and talking to it while she got a close-up shot with her instamatic camera. The humungous moose ignored both of them and continued to munch the purple wildflower blossoms, taking no interest whatsoever in the crazy photographers.

When rain threatened as we pulled out our 4′ x 6′ tent, Rob demonstrated his procedure for trenching around our sleeping spot to keep rain from seeping in at the bottom. We were impressed, and although we had no rain that night, we followed his reliable technique several times and saved ourselves from some nasty wet nights.

International Students. The Snake River became our escort again between the Tetons and Yellowstone when we got going the next day. We rode along a parkway for 5 or 6 miles—a lovely section of forested hills just before the south entrance to Yellowstone. The hills and headwinds were not cooperating, so we knew we wouldn't make it into the park until the following afternoon. We were counting on a recreation area marked along the parkway for our last night before Yellowstone, hoping it would be empty. After circling slowly through the grounds we realized every camp was filled, again. We were feeling discouraged and seriously considered sneaking into an out of the way spot. Then:

"Hello...Hello...yes, here?" We were surprised, not expecting to hear anyone speaking to us, but there he was, a young man with a mop of thick black hair and glasses gesturing for us to come up the trail to his car.

"You...can...camp...here...with us," he said in a heavy accent. We caught up with them, a Japanese couple, not sure at first how much English they understood. After all the miles we had traveled and all the kindness we had experienced, it still took us a second to open up. It turned out they were a little reserved, too, but friendly.

Foreign students Rioji Yamaguchi and his wife, Yoki, had been studying in Oregon for one year. They explained that, to get more of an authentic feel for the American experience, they decided to move to Sheridan, Wyoming, and live the Western lifestyle they hoped to find there. Yoki was very shy and quiet, but she completely opened up their space to us, using gracious gestures, and invited us to share a delicious meal as she fried four trout Rioji had just fished out of the river. I mixed up pan biscuits to add to the plates, making it a truly international camping feast. Later, Rioji took Paul down to the water for his first-ever fishing lesson. He had never used a fishing pole and took instructions with interest. Once Paul had pulled a live rainbow trout from the water, he told me he could never be a fisherman at heart. We all had a good laugh at that. The Yamaguchis had all of their belongings packed into their car where they slept comfortably. Paul and I thanked them for their hospitality and crawled into our tent by the side of their space. Before parting ways in the morning, we invited them to join us at the campsites we had reserved in Yellowstone.

Yellowstone National Park. We rode through the gate into Yellowstone, the first national park established just over 100 years ago, encompassing over 3,000 square miles. It was exciting to be there—but nothing, absolutely nothing prepared me for what I was about to experience. I wondered about the bear population as I noted signs warning people:

VIEW WILDLIFE FROM YOUR CAR.

We had been steadily climbing since Jackson Hole and I became aware of the beauty surrounding us. The high country air was crystalline and the mountains created a dizzying circle—nothing but slopes and peaks blanketed by rich green forest.

The road ahead and behind was steep and steady, leading me further into the enchantment. For that first day in the park, there was nothing to interrupt the lush green and granite natural environment. No fences or buildings, no concessions, only the constant stream of automobiles and camper-trailers driving past on their way to enjoy the park—going faster and surely seeing less from their car windows than we could from our bikes. It was 25 miles to the first of our reserved campsites. Before we camped we reached our first crossing of the Continental Divide.

"Can you imagine? From the point of view of flowing water, this is the highest point on the continent," Paul exclaimed. "From here, it all divides in half, flowing from here down the Snake, Columbia, and into the Pacific. And then, from this side, it goes down the Yellowstone, the Missouri, to the Mississippi rivers and the Atlantic! Just think of it, in a car it would be something, but we're crossing the Divide on bicycles. How did we ever get here?" The impact of our trip suddenly hit me—a transcontinental bicycle ride and there we were, standing on the backbone of the entire continent. We had ridden to the top of the world.

Just as we had learned on our first slight grade in California and then over Teton Pass: climbing hills and climbing mountains involved really nothing more than pushing one pedal stroke after another, resting when we needed to and—most of all—simply wanting to get to the top. Riding the high country in one of the grandest national parks, absorbing as much as possible, we scarcely had time to think about the work our bodies were doing.

Journal Entry ~ August 6, 1974 The ground is pretty unstable so there's a raised boardwalk built across Geyser Basin to walk on and get a closer view. The churning water is probably 170 degrees, bubbles come from rising carbon dioxide. This amazing stuff comes out of holes one or two miles below the surface of the earth at the magma layer where heat is transferred through the rocks. The water is really pure even though it smells weird and acrid. I am baffled by what's happening right under our feet. Yellowstone—suspended in time since prehistoric days when the earth was just forming, simple life forms born from raw elements: fire, water, air, earth. Just imagine early humans and first explorers stumbling upon this mysterious place—with no experience or explanation—must have been quite frightening, awe-inspiring. Along with thousands of other visitors, I am amazed and dizzy trying to comprehend the beauty in the depths of Morning Glory Pool, the bubbling mud pots, the explosive Old Faithful Geyser.

Yellowstone Lake. Yellowstone Lake, the highest large lake on the continent, sits at 7,733 feet elevation. Our campground was right on the shore of West Thumb, practically at the edge of the water. The ancient forest, left as nature intended, provided a gorgeous, private spot to settle in. Paul and I arrived, and eventually Rob Mearling and the Yamaguchis found their way to our camp.

It was quite an experience when we introduced the outgoing, effervescent Berkeley traveler and the reserved, polite Japanese couple. Each one of us added our unique characters and lifestyles to create a little family for a couple of nights. Two hopeful and enthusiastic students from a faraway country, a progressive adventuring storyteller from Berkeley, and a newly married couple out to conquer the next bend in the road on four wheels. It was a special evening, contrasting personalities with diverse ways of communicating. Rioji caught enough fish for Yoki to fry into a grand feast. Rob brewed freshly ground coffee and mixed mocha with his unique portable espresso pot. Paul and I contributed canned beans and I stirred up a batch of Bisquik with oatmeal for a special cookie treat. We spun yarns of mountainous adventures and feats of the days' rides and treks.

The dark woods were closing in, we heard the sounds of nature around us as evening approached. Clouds and thunder threatened until a rainbow over the lake graced the setting sun. Rangers' cars passed with loudspeakers warning about bears in the night. They demanded everyone carry flashlights to the restrooms, don't walk around alone, and most of all, do not leave food around to attract wild animals. "Enjoy your night in Yellowstone," they concluded.

We saw no bears. But the next morning and for three more days—hot springs, waterfalls, geysers, and lava mountains filled our view. In Yellowstone a person can stand closer to the center of the earth than anywhere else.

Journal Entry ~ August 10, 1974 Last evening at Fishing Bridge, we were standing together just looking out across the expanse of lake. Someone at the next campsite turned their radio up loud and we all listened as President Nixon gave his resignation speech. Everyone heard what sounded like justification—he never actually admitted that he betrayed the country by influencing the election; he said he's not a quitter. He dragged the country through the Watergate break-in, a coverup, and lies to influence the election. I am genuinely relieved that this guy is done being president. A bunch of emotions swirling through me. I'm trying to see how Paul and I fit into this moment in history. Standing here, in the midst of geyser basins and Yellowstone's grandeur, 2000 miles from home, I can see the bigger picture. It's that broader view I was craving. Now I see a lot more clearly. We're just a part of the whole. One man's failings. Two bikers' conquest of a mountain. Natural forces shaping the geography and geology of the earth we inhabit. Everything is possible. We get to choose which events shape us and guide us. Now I have a better perspective than if I'd heard this speech three months earlier. Nixon's crimes appear as a mere blip that barely registers in importance to the whole. I am ready to move on.

The magnificent Grand Canyon of the Yellowstone was next. This gorgeous, wild river had its beginnings at the Continental Divide in northwestern Wyoming, slicing its way through eons of historical layers of earth, opening beauty and wonder in its path. Writers, painters, and early photographers journeyed to this place to capture the lights, shades, sounds, and textures of the river. Thomas Moran's oil painting reproduced the drama of Inspiration Point, which was indeed an inspiration for the eventual creation of this, the first national park. Here, I also discovered the reason behind the name "Yellow Stone" in the sheer golden-hued cliffs of the canyon.

Sylvan Pass. We headed uphill toward Yellowstone's eastern boundary at 7700 feet and were about to face another steep climb over Sylvan Pass at 8500 feet. As we exited the park a ranger warned us about a lone female black bear who apparently found it amusing to pop out of the woods to surprise travelers. She told us to be on the lookout but then assured us we wouldn't be in any danger. We were a bit wary, riding through the quiet morning without many cars or other travelers. The only wildlife we saw was a family of deer grazing off the side of the road and a forest full of birds chirping their early morning songs, seeking out their bird breakfast before the gathering clouds broke into a storm.

It was still August, but at the top of the pass we were surprised to find patches of snow. After the climb, I held on tight to the handlebars on another careening, insane descent at top speeds in freezing, driving rain. I couldn't see anything but the front of my bike. My red nylon parka flapped at my nose and mouth, spilling water up into my face till I couldn't keep my eyes open. Hands frozen to the handlebars and gripping with all the strength I could muster, I was a two-wheeled runaway holding on for dear life. The last 10 miles of Yellowstone National Park were steep, fast, and hazy images flashing by and we sped past the exit gate in a blur.

Cody, Wyoming. After our terrifying downhill exit from the park, at a mountain hunting lodge appropriately called Buffalo Bill's, we climbed off the bikes for cups of hot coffee to warm our hands and calm our nerves. We could have easily spent $20 for an overnight indoor cabin, but it was still early afternoon and the town of Cody was just 40 miles ahead. The conversation in my head went as expected: *"Should we think about stopping here where it's warm and dry? No, we need to keep riding. Can't let this much of the day go by without getting anywhere. But it might rain again and I really don't want to. But we must..."*

So we mounted up, saddles still damp and packs still dripping from the last downpour and pushed on down the road again. If every time one of us wanted to stop and the other agreed, we'd never make it in one summer. Paul and I tempered each other's fears and reluctance with lots of encouragement, reminding each other every once in awhile that we really did want to take this trip and to do that we needed to keep on riding.

Twenty miles outside of Cody, away from cars, people, farms, and towns, we pulled off into a gravel drive that led deep into antelope grazing country. We watched as a great herd of pronghorns pranced off in the distance, running toward the foothills. Wyoming wasn't flat, as we had expected, but it was definitely deserted and seemingly endless. Our morning breaks had changed slightly—now featuring a bag of cookies instead of the usual milk and donuts since stores were few and far between. We sat for awhile on the ground, enjoying our snack as the sun warmed our tanned legs.

"How on earth did we get here? We're halfway to the Atlantic Ocean, traveling on just our fragile bikes, all alone together!" I said.

Paul agreed, "Can you believe it? There's not another soul within 40 miles of us right now."

"I know! And here we sit, perfectly comfortable in the middle of the road munching on cookies. What are we doing here?" I reflected. "Remember on the coast, we saw tons of bikers going North and South along Highway 1. We only met a few on the Columbia River. And then we saw that big group of hikers from New York in Yellowstone."

"Right! But now, I wonder if we'll see any more crazy people on bicycles out here in the middle of nowhere. Do you know how lucky we are, to be this free and able to do this?"

Resting on the deserted pavement, I considered the thousands of special moments that had passed: the rainy nights, windy days, and glorious downhill rides. All the unique little towns we'd ridden into and become a part of for an hour or two; all the faces, the cars, the miles and miles of highway we'd traveled. The wonders of nature, the landforms were becoming an essential part of me, written in the crevices of my hands steering the handlebars, rippling through thigh muscles, creases in the bend of knees and ankles churning through the country. Every inch of land belonged to me—the intimate perspective from a bike saddle required that I notice everything. Being vitally active, strong, healthy, relaxed, and smiling most of the time brought the beauty of this ride into sharp focus.

Rock Formations. The weather improved and we passed a couple of campgrounds but continued on since the sun was beginning to pop through. Around 3:00 we stopped along the Shoshone River in a forested wilderness area and found a quiet place to stay the night. A magical setting sheltered within a solid rock canyon where the walls towered high above us and opened into a skylight revealing a slice of bright blue. Red-brown and darker red stones curved into spires and pillars. Fanciful shapes balanced precariously on tops of the pinnacles. I imagined faces and forms in the rocks and wind caves and found many silhouettes had names: Duck Rock, the Holy City, Old Woman and House.

We learned the delicate-looking rock was a hard kind of agglomerate mosaic of multicolored stones that had solidified in remnants from volcanic lava. Centuries of wind and water elements had taken their hand to create a masterpiece of art and beauty over miles of canyon walls. A tired, relieved couple of bikers rested that night in the enchanting forest camp, deserted save for us. The river rushed and gurgled its way past the front of our tent on its way to the Atlantic. My exhausted body rested, secure in the triumph of having crossed the Rockies—but, as it turned out, I was floating on a false cloud of contentment. The most challenging mountain climb was not, as I believed, at our backs!

Journal Entry ~ August 12, 1974 A lot has happened since we left Santa Barbara. The ocean seems far away, almost as far as the moon. And those dreaded mountains behind us are forever engraved in our hearts and memories. Countless people we had never expected to meet are truly the soul of our ride as they stay close in our hearts and minds. I'm thinking about the skeptics back home who figured we'd probably never get past the first hill. Here we are, on the east side of the Rockies. I can bask in the encouragement we received from Mrs. Granden, the enthusiastic bicycling family in Oregon, even store clerks wishing us well. Every person we met on the road seemed happy to stop whatever they were doing at that moment and take the time to speak with us, ask about our trip, tell us about their lives, share their own hopes and dreams. We would never have met them if we had not set out on our bikes to see what we could see.

We were on our way to Sheridan. We spent the night in a tiny spot on the map called Greybull, hardly even a town except for an A&W Root Beer stand and a collection of abandoned rusty cars and trucks. We met two bikers coming from the direction we were headed. In their faces we read the trials and steep grades of a big hill. They were buoyant and enthusiastic as we chatted, laughing about the downhill ride still fresh in their minds. But they did not have many encouraging words for us facing the uphill side. It had been difficult riding for them, they told us. But then they countered with a happy description of flat, straight and level miles in South Dakota and Minnesota—on the far side of the Bighorn Mountains.

So, we awoke early the next morning, mounted up and set off to face our next challenge. We ended up riding side by side, talking about our dads back home on the East and West coasts, imagining how they must surely be impressed and proud, seeing their kids being so brave and capable. Someone in Greybull had described the pass to be 25 miles, climbing from 4000 feet to 9000 feet beginning with three long switchbacks. Brave, indeed!

The Bighorns ~ Granite Pass. We quickly came up on the base of the mountain that threatened to block our path, slanting right up out of the broad, flat plain. First were reddish mounds and spires and eventually we were surrounded by solid rock as we began the climb. Little twinges of hesitation shot through my gut when I began noticing the cliff at the edge of the road. The switchbacks came all at once. Nothing to do but dive on in and begin the climb.

A sunny morning encouraged our uphill start. Switchbacks, as described by seasoned bicyclists, were supposed to be the easiest to climb because you could see your progress and feel the accomplishment at each turn. I forced every ounce of muscle power into every downstroke. I hoped to gain some sense of accomplishment for facing another difficult climb. Drivers and passengers alike cheered us on through their open windows as they passed. A family of kids, piled against the rear window of a station wagon, waved and stared out at us. A travel-trailer blared past and broke our concentration, shouting on their CB loud speaker, "HANG IN THERE! KEEP ON TRUCKIN'!"

We climbed, and turned. Climbed, and turned. The sun disappeared behind ominous gray cloud cover as we came upon a road construction sign warning of 3 miles of gravel roadbed ahead. The road became increasingly steeper, the surface was mostly sandy. We pushed on through loose gravel, and for the first time I regretted the presence of my rear packs laden with 30 pounds of gear. Trucks grinding past forced us too close to the cliff and into deeper gravel. At one point it was simply too grueling to navigate from the saddle, so I dismounted and pushed the bike until I reached a firmer surface to ride on. Then the wind rose up through the canyon, howling and icy cold.

The sloping path ahead revealed only more mountain. Rough granite outcroppings pushed out of the highest inclines, resembling great temples and pyramids. Our experience so far in mountainous terrain was that a road normally followed a river cut, and we were on the lookout for a shallower path between the steep walls. All we could make out were more peaks ahead.

Flagmen along the construction zone were unsympathetic, telling us we had only a mile or two to the end. We pushed hard for four exhausting hours under gray skies, finding no possible places to break for lunch, seething leg pains slowing me down; we were both exhausted. Paul spotted a sign for a camp, but it was 21 miles off the main road down a muddy, rutted drive. We decided against going the extra distance, and at last I noticed a small ravine protected from traffic by a huge rock next to the roadway. Lunch was not satisfying, not enough to replenish the energy we were expending. It was 4 p.m. and I was too stiff to stand. Even though it was too early in the day, I was ready to stop and sleep on the side of the road.

After the late lunch, we passed the construction and traffic was lighter. We came upon some free-range cattle and slowed as a black mother cow on one side of the road crossed in front of us to reach her calf on the other side. The light was fading. Rain threatened. Eventually we came upon ski lifts and runs chopped through the forest. The ski area was deserted, but I fantasized about a lodge with a blazing fire. Not long after that, the trees thinned out and I realized we were above the timberline. Wind was with us, then against us. Haze and clouds hung low over my head and the rain came down in cold sheets, blasting against my parka.

And then, there it was—the top of the pass at 8,950 feet. We'd conquered the mountain—and were rewarded with a freezing torrent of water dumping on us, making the road nearly invisible. I could not see ahead through raindrops and tears of exhaustion. And then we were on our way down—quaking joints and speeding bikes on a slick, darkening road. We spun, slipped, and slid down into the icy, freezing storm until we came upon a welcome sight: a log-built diner with the lights on!

Dripping wet, we burst through the heavy doors and found ourselves in a small one-room café with a pool table, an outhouse, and a bit of smoldering wood in the fireplace where I could dry out my socks. They had frozen pizza and hot coffee so we sat and thawed out and watched on the small TV as the newly-seated president Gerald Ford gave his first address to Congress and pardoned Nixon. I was too numbed by the riding experience to make much meaning out of his speech.

There was nowhere to stay the night except in the forest. A couple of jokers playing cards tried to tell me that the bull elk out on Granite Pass have been known to chase people and leave them gored by the side of the road. I was tougher than to let that bother me. I had just propelled myself up that pass on my bike and nothing as remote as the threat of bull elk in the night was going to scare me.

We climbed back on the bikes before dusk, feeling a little sore, but we wanted to explore the road that would take us down the mountain the next day. Sunset broke through the storm at the summit and we found a level piece of dirt at the top, a deserted picnic area and a lean-to for shelter. We set up the tent and were quickly unconscious to the world, the bikes, and everything but each other—cuddled warm and safe inside our sleeping bags.

Morning sunshine dappled through the pines and roused us out of sleep. We gulped down our granola breakfast, then took a moment to readjust my derailleur after the punishing gravel ride from the day before. Anxious to find out what was ahead, we gathered up our gear and took off. The range we were on seemed unbelievably high. Just gazing across at the expanse of peaks was impressive. Colors came into sharp focus in the pristine air. I had never seen such clarity and beauty in the greens, golds, and bright white clouds against the deep blue of the sky. As I rounded a slope and came to the eastern side of the Bighorns I had an uninterrupted panoramic view looking across to the horizon, the exquisite sky melting into the sunrise at the edge of the world. A few thousand feet below, the whole eastern half of the country stretched out in front of us—flat, wide, and open. We stopped at the crest so Paul could get a picture between rock walls of the pass and out to the prairies of Eastern Wyoming and South Dakota.

"We've seen where the sun sets in the West. Now we'll go catch the sunrise!" he exclaimed.

We did not hesitate. We headed downhill.

My bike truly took wings at that moment and flew me down the side of that mountain. As Paul sped past me I heard him singing, "I'm flying! I'm flying!" For more than twenty miles we coasted down wide curves and sharp switchbacks. I let go of the brakes and sensed throughout every cell in my body the ecstasy of wind and sun and motion. That was the reward for the agony of the previous day's climb. I would not forget this feeling of freedom—me and my bike, and the open sky.

Journal Entry ~ August 13, 1974
Fly free bicycle
lifted up
I am light—let go
nothing touching nothing
and breeze by—the universe
tree gust stones sky branch air
hum cloud cool
smile
touch again down

7 Meeting Challenges

2024 Reflections

As we rode all those miles across the continent in the first months of marriage, we naturally kept an eye out for places we might want to live. I won't call it "places to settle down" since that's not something Paul and I really ever want to do, even today. But we realized there ought to be a job, a house, and a place to call home. Where would we go? What could we do? Dozens of possibilities crossed our minds over the 10 states we traversed. Maybe we'd choose a coastal cliff house near Mendocino. We could start a redwood tree farm or grow and sell Christmas trees. A cozy cabin along the Columbia or the Snake might be an adventure. Paul would love to open a photo studio near national parks and mountains. I wouldn't mind converting an abandoned railroad station somewhere out on the prairie. We might live on a farm or open a basement bike shop—there was no end to our ideas.

We have lived in a variety of locations over the years, including a couple of favorite spots from our biking trip. After resting up for a couple of months back east and then in Santa Barbara, we spent three years (1975-1977) in San Francisco—perched up on Telegraph Hill in a great little apartment with a view of the Bay Bridge. Those hills were fun to skip down, but too crazy steep to ride very much. We didn't have a lot of space for growing vegetables, or growing a family, but we often rode the MUNI bus out to the Golden Gate Park archery field with our bows and arrows.

After life in the cosmopolitan city, the thought of Portland, Oregon, tempted us. In 1977, we set out to see how we'd enjoy living in a peaceful place with lots of rainy days for gardening and a view of all those volcanoes. Paul found a job, I found a house, and in another year we were expecting our first child. What I was *not* expecting was how childbirth would revive memories of the bike trip during labor on the day our daughter was coming into this world.

Finding Strength. The comparison makes sense to me now. I can totally understand how bicycling over mountain passes really had prepared me for doing the hard physical work of childbirth. Before our children were born, my most difficult challenge was pushing the bicycle up over the Bighorn Mountains. I knew what strength I had inside; I had discovered it at the summit of Granite Pass. My birth-coach midwife was a naturopathic doctor who believed in being prepared. She coached me through yoga practice and taught me how to tap into my physical strength while finding my center to relax into the effort.

Paul was right there, he walked with me through three days of contractions and held my hands attentively over 11 hours of hard labor until the moment of joy when he held our daughter in his arms. It was absolutely the same kind of hard work as biking through my physical limits up those mountains, and both experiences came with a huge reward. Seeing the far horizon from the top of a mountain is much like the first time gazing into the eyes of your child—inspiring a world full of possibilities.

Three years later, back in Southern California, the birth of our second child was easier than climbing up a 9,000-foot mountain, as most second births seem to be. As our son grew, I called upon another aspect of our bicycling experience. He sought the same thrill of freedom and adventure when as a young teen he decided to compete in the exhilarating, challenging world of downhill mountain bike racing. After all, his parents had biked across the country under our own power, stretching our limits and pushing beyond our abilities to find what was out there. I was thrilled to encourage our son and watch how he would stretch his own limits and discover for himself what the world has to offer.

A River and A Mountain. Paul and I have never lost our deep connection with nature. We gave our children names to forever remember that connection: Brandywine, named for a gentle river that flows through New York, Pennsylvania, and on to Delaware; Sierra for the mountain Range of Light that traverses California north to south. I see how our daughter has inherited my strength and the steadiness of a river, adding her own inner grace as she pursues her dreams and guides her family's growth. She has revived a nostalgic lunch counter featuring her own handmade ice cream, and her creative diner space is a center of community joy and delight. Our son takes after Paul, supporting his family while capturing beauty in visual images as he elevates that photographic talent to another level. Running a creative arts magazine, he pulls together local stories, remarkable artworks, and striking photography to highlight the authentic voices in his community.

We're counting on our grandchildren to continue the family bicycling tradition. Each of the three started out on balance bikes. Bodhi rides to school with his dad, Suzie is learning better balance on her two-wheeler over the summer with her parents, and Angus catches a ride with his mom every morning in her electric-powered cargo bike nicknamed "The Gup." They're happily on their way to bigger and better adventures.

Life Is A Bike Ride. It's no secret that physical activity promotes health and well-being. In these climate-changing times, studies focus on the positive effects of the biking lifestyle. Researchers have recently identified measurable impact on the common good in cities and communities where residents frequently use bicycles for transportation. Biking allows more opportunity for social interaction, encourages caring and helpfulness, and creates a stronger sense of neighborhood and community. I'm all for that—more compassion and more human contact, just like the days when we explored the whole country on our bikes.

There is an undeniable benefit when bike transportation reduces the carbon footprint and helps make progress toward a healthier planet. Bicycle manufacturing companies are making note of the changing environment where the switch to bike riding will be a significant step toward sustainability. Bicyclists share values that reinforce my hope for the future.

Bike Physics. Just imagine being suspended in a timeless moment of joy at the top of a mountain after a long climb. Think of the sense of power a biker feels the moment the crest of a hill is in sight, or the spine-tingling sensation of speed, rolling along through uninterrupted miles of flat open spaces. I think of my everyday life like that, rolling through the ups and downs, never knowing what lies ahead on the road I'm traveling. It helps to remember that I'm traveling under my own effort, and because it's about me making the effort, I can face life's challenges and roll through the bumps in the road.

I still wonder at the amazing physics of biking. I can absolutely feel the thrill of riding any time I'm astride my bicycle. How does that happen? What brings me to that joyful feeling of bliss on a bicycle?

What happens on the bike when rolling resistance meets the earth's gravitational force as you approach the crest of a hill? It's nearly indescribable, experiencing the natural surge of speed and propulsion that occurs just at the top. You're pushing the bike against gravity—you have a sensation of lift when those forces meet, the weightlessness is real. It's a little like riding a roller coaster, but the difference is that you've done the work yourself, and the reward is all that much sweeter.

What if you could feel that transformation every time you practice any kind of physical activity, just let go, do the hard work, relax into the flow, and believe that the combined goals of feeling great and connecting with nature are within reach. I crave that sensation and I know it's just a matter of going outside and getting on the bicycle.

When you reach that perfect balance—in the instant when your level of skill meets the difficulty of the challenge—you experience a heightened level of satisfaction. I used to think it was only endorphins, chemicals released when the body experiences stress during exercise or physical exertion, increasing the flow of oxygen to the brain. Now I know, it's about the physics of the bike. About the weightlessness at the top of a rise. It's science, and it's magical.

8  PLAINS

Wyoming . South Dakota

At the eastern foot of the Rocky Mountains the country opens to a dramatic landscape of mostly flat, gentle prairie. The high plains formed when rivers flowing out of the mountains deposited eons of sediment across great expanses of land. A 360-degree view of open, uninterrupted grasslands encircled us. The riding here would be desolate, an abrupt change after coming out of the high country and the dramatic scenery behind us. Even with all we had seen so far, we were really only experiencing a narrow strip of the country, barely a glimpse of all the *un*seen places that lay beyond the horizon.

Sheridan, Wyoming, was a little bigger than many of our recent stops. We treated ourselves to hamburgers and chocolate cake in celebration of our thrilling downhill rush out of the Bighorns. We located the post office to pick up our General Delivery mail. That night at a roadside rest area we enjoyed snacks from home while reading letters and notes from our families. We tried to get some sleep but were, instead, entertained by our first experience with desert heat lightning—crackling, crashing bursts of light flashed inside the low clouds and kept us both on edge all night.

The next day, Paul saw on the map that the road heading east actually curved north and would bring us within 15 miles of the Montana border. We talked about adding another state to our itinerary, but neither of us had the energy to go out of the way just to say we had. We passed rolling, empty countryside dotted with sagebrush and grasslands and an occasional farm or a herd of horses. Horses always stopped grazing and looked up to keep an eye on the strange creatures as we cruised by. A headwind rose up and got stronger as we went, blowing constantly in our faces all day.

The next town, which was pretty much a one-store place called Ucross, offered a place for a short break. A man named Buck owned the store and likely the entire town, judging by the signs on the buildings. We stopped and bought candy bars from Buck himself, a weathered old guy sporting a full gray head of hair and scraggly beard. He greeted us with a tip of his cowboy hat and didn't say much of anything after greeting us with, "Howdy." We hung out for a bit to admire the wall decorated with portraits of Buck on safari, posing with his conquests—several big cats and one elephant. There was an opportunity to stay over at Buck's Campground and Trailer Park, but we were anxious to get further down the road to see if we could find someplace more to our liking. An hour or so later we hit the jackpot, but didn't realize it until later that evening.

Clearmont. We spotted the water tower from a few miles out as the road took us right through the slightly larger town of Clearmont. As we got closer we noticed there were a few more trees, a couple of side streets, and a small café right in the middle of town called The Red Arrow. We pulled in to ask about camping spots and found Fern, the proprietor, who explained she had a few cabins in back for rent for only

$5 a night. For a couple of weeks Paul and I had been thinking it would be nice to take a real break from riding. The last place we had more than a day off the bikes was San Francisco. We found this to be a laid-back, friendly gathering place full of character and interesting people, so we took a room for two nights to wait out the wind and get to know more about life in Wyoming. We settled in at Cabin #4 and headed back to the café for dinner.

"You two really ridin' your bicycles to the East Coast?" The waitress came in from the back with wet hair wrapped in a towel. Her clothes were casual, an oversized white t-shirt and red cotton pants. She grabbed an apron from behind the counter as she came to our table. "Sorry, I was in the shower. You folks are a little earlier than the regular customers."

"Yes, we're riding bikes, all the way." Paul answered.

"Wow, aren't you tired? I could never do that!" she replied while pouring coffee into two thick mugs.

"Well, yes. We are kinda tired. That's why we decided to rest up here for a day or two," I told her. "What's it like living in Clearmont, Wyoming, anyway? What do you all do here?"

"Oh," she said. "I like it here. Used to live in Colorado. I'm from Detroit. I tried to get a teaching job in Colorado, but the rent was too high and I couldn't get a job there—had to live in my tent in a vacant lot. One night when I got snowed in I figured out I had to leave and come here. I've actually applied for a job in Sheridan and have an appointment this week with the school board."

"What about the school here in Clearmont?" I asked. "Didn't we pass a high school down the road?"

"Yeah, I was up for a job here for next year, but something happened and I'm not going to get it. I hope this one in Sheridan works out," she said. "Where are you guys going after you get back east?"

Paul took a thoughtful moment to sip his coffee and then answered, "We'll stay there awhile, and see what we can figure out after this trip is over. There are a lot of places we could go."

In a few minutes a cowboy sauntered in, ordered ham and eggs, and talked with us a bit about antelope hunting out of season. He also explained to us how the coal and oil industry was really taking over ranching in Wyoming. We sat around for the rest of the afternoon as others came in and out and we got to meet most of the people living in and around Clearmont. Everyone seemed to stop by the diner in their pickups on the way home after a day's work or in the mornings on their way out to the ranch. As it turned out, through word of mouth everyone in three or four neighboring towns heard about us, too. Eventually, Paul and I headed back to our cabin and sat out on the wood porch to watch the sun go down as kids played outdoors on that peaceful summer evening.

The one-room cabin was quite luxurious to our way of thinking. It had a bathroom, a comfortable bed, and walls and a roof to protect us from weather. We slept in and had breakfast at the café each morning. We hung out with Chester the German Shepherd who liked to sit on the hood of a car out front. In the afternoon we walked around town to explore the neighborhood, the old white church, and the train depot. Later, Paul sat outside whittling away at some driftwood he had started working on along the Pacific Coast. I finally had a bit of quiet time to write down some of the thoughts that had been forming so far on our travels.

Sharing Thoughts. Relaxing for two days off the bikes, we had a chance to reflect on the trip and share some deeper feelings.

"I really can't stop thinking about Yellowstone," I said. "There's so much going on with the geology and forces that shaped the earth, I had no idea. The thermal basins and steaming mud pots were my favorite—sort of mystical how it all burbles up in that one place."

Paul smiled back at me. "The whole trip is like that, a lot to learn about. Like geography, how the land is formed and how it affects our riding. Our unique position on the bikes and pedaling every mile makes me aware of the lay of the land. There's an uphill—why is it in our path right there? How much of the valleys and canyons we ride through were created by rivers, or ancient seas? It's all pretty incredible."

"This kind of exploring reminds me of how you always used to take me on dates to discover something new, something pretty to see, a new beach or a hike in the foothills near Santa Barbara. Only this way, on the bikes, we have a better advantage, to see more up close."

I had been intrigued with the adventures he took me on even before we set off on this trip. There was always a surprise in store on those outings and he was still surprising me every day.

"You're right," Paul said. "Time passes by slowly while we're going uphill—so we have a chance to think about where a mountain range came from. And then we met the challenge of that hill, and coasting down, rocks and cliffs rush by so close to the body, it's easy to be curious and wonder what's happening geologically with the dirt literally flying by us."

I considered the questions we asked each other every time we came upon a new, unbelievable sight.

"There are so many things I don't know about. It's always so much fun with you, coming up with questions and trying to figure out the answers. That's gotta be another whole project when we stop traveling—to search libraries and books to try to find out more about the land, the canyons, and passes we're riding through."

Then Paul remarked, "I guess you can go through the libraries while I work on all the negatives once we get to my folks' place. I am going to have a bunch of pictures to sort through!"

"I still can't believe we rode the bikes over those 9,000-foot mountains! That pass really did me in! But just think about where we started from—and that view when we came over the top—it seemed like I could literally see all the way to New York. No more mountain barriers between us and the East Coast."

The second morning at the Red Arrow, Paul spread out the map and found the next town we could stop for supplies would be Gillette, 65 miles away. We left the mountainous part of Wyoming behind and rode away from our rest days in Clearmont with renewed energy. My spirit stretched out across the unbroken scenery, riding the black ribbon of road through the barren landscape wherever it led. The thought of discovery rekindled my imagination. At times we were completely alone out on the prairie, yet I felt confident that the rest of the trip would be smooth sailing on flat, straight roads. Plenty to explore and nothing to indicate we'd run into any problems, even with a long ride ahead.

Journal Entry ~ August 16, 1974 A hundred grasshoppers in the sage. Wind and chirping crickets and rustling weeds are the only sound. We just crossed the Powder River. The locals say it's "a mile wide and an inch deep." Way off to our right the southern peaks of the Bighorns fade into a bluish haze. But here in a full circle around us the land stretches out in ten different shades of brown. No shadows now in the late morning—only hills sifting down to smooth mounds after withstanding decades of prairie winds and storms rolling across them. I always thought I hated desert. But now I'm beginning to feel I cannot dislike any part of this land—it's all part of the whole that we're trying to absorb and understand.

Feeling the effects of the extended drought that had gripped the area, we pedaled out of town early. It didn't take long for the heat to settle in, there wasn't much of a breeze to cool the sweat collecting on my arms and dripping down my back. I told myself that if the ride got too difficult we could stop at Spotted Horse, a small town appearing on the map halfway to Gillette. I drank sparingly and looked forward to refilling our water supply. Maybe we'd even snag some ice cream.

I was counting on quenching my thirst but Spotted Horse didn't have much to offer. We saw a historical marker at the crest of the next hill and a small sign pointed to a building across the street that read: "Spotted Horse." That was it; nothing but dead grass and a crooked, run-down shack. Paint was peeling off the sides. A rusty old gas pump stood out front. The annoying little man inside sold only beer and sandwiches. Paul checked the shelves to see what he could find, and I walked over to a spigot by the gas pump to fill the water bottles. I poured out the last drips from our two-quart bottle and tried the faucet. Nothing came out. The water pipe was dry. Spotted Horse had no running water! The rude proprietor informed us he had only his personal stash and he was not about to part with any of his water. He had beer to sell or nothing. Most people we met so far had been remarkably kind and helpful but this guy's attitude was such a contrast. We turned down the beer and continued on.

The afternoon turned into a worrisome 35 miles of desolation, with only enough water to occasionally moisten my parched lips. All along, Paul had been praising the beauty and serenity of the open and empty Plains states. I should have learned by now not to be discouraged by much at that point. But the wind-worn hills and parched grassland began to wear me down.

We pushed on—thirsty, discouraged, and knowing that we could not stop until we got to the next town since without replenishing our water supply we would not be able to cook at camp. I tried hard to appreciate the colorful views in the distance as the sun dropped to a low angle behind us. Mostly, I was desperate for civilization. When we finally came to an occupied building on the outskirts of Gillette we stopped and begged for water from a couple of teenage kids working a construction headquarters. They couldn't quite comprehend why we were on bicycles, how we got there, and how desperate we were for a drink. But they were friendly, let us fill our water bottles, and showed us the Coke machine where we could quench our thirst.

It was an uphill ride into Gillette and the campground was right there, a big sign pointed us to the camp that was only open during camping hours—6 p.m. to 10 a.m. Paul noticed my front tire gumwall was bulging in two spots and the tube was ready to blow. I was feeling lucky that he saw it while we were in a town with a bike store, but the bike store was located in the owner's home and the owner had just gotten up when we knocked. Said he wasn't open yet. We found a Western Auto shop that happened to have a cheap bike tire, but at least it was the right size. After laundry and donuts, we didn't get going that day until almost noon.

We rode by an open-pit coal mine at Wyodak, where coal was scraped from a 50-foot vein under the surface. The coal was mined, crushed, sized, and treated before being loaded on train cars and transported, supplying power for the Black Hills area of the state. The mining operation had left an unsightly scar on the land. Towns were scarce and the days continued to be sunny and warm so we rode along across the tawny golden sea of grass. Small communities dotted the landscape like isolated islands in that sea; when we asked for information about what was ahead, where we might camp or find supplies, locals did not seem to know much beyond the town they lived in.

Carnival. It took some doing to find anyone to ask permission to camp at the town park in Upton. The police station was closed and someone told us they had only one policeman so we spent an hour trying to track him down. He wasn't at the station, not at the café, not in the saloon, and no sign of him patrolling. Paul went into a noisy restaurant to try calling his folks. Meanwhile, I watched as a traveling carnival was being unloaded from three dusty, rusty trucks in an empty lot. A trailer opened into a concession stand and half a dozen rough-and-tumble carnival workers set up four rides, including a colorful creaky old Ferris wheel. As dusk fell and darkened the sky, lights flashed on and pipe organ music blared. Little boys and girls poured noisily out of houses and a few teens drove up in cars and pickups.

Eventually the town cop cruised by so I waved him down to ask about camping in the park. First thing I noticed was a rifle lying across the front seat. He wasn't wearing a uniform. But he was friendly enough and drawled "Yep, that's fine to camp in the park." We chatted for a minute. He told me he was from St. Louis. Upton had only three people on the police force, because nothing ever happened there and he was anxious to get back home where there was more to do. Then he confided that he'd maybe like to make a bicycle trip someday.

The carnival energy was high for the folks in Upton. It fascinated me to see the way a caravan of temporary stalls and rickety roller coaster rides traveled around to these isolated communities over the summer. A bunch of carnies living on the road, sort of like us, but towing trailers and cotton-candy machines to entertain the scattered population on warm summer evenings. Thankfully, the festival of music and lights didn't keep us awake as we hit the tent soon after supper and, exhausted as usual, slept through the noise.

Wind was blowing against us, and when we spotted another one-street town, Osage, we pulled off for a break. Curley's Bar was the only place open on Sunday and music inside attracted us, so we had a couple beers and got to know a little about the bartender. His daughter had lived in California, and he admitted he might like to try living there at some point.

We enjoyed our beer and then, walking out into the heat and climbing back on the bike, I felt slightly lightheaded. As we drifted down the deserted road we both got a bit giggly in the bright, hot sun. Paul was being silly and suddenly he burst out singing Paul Simon's "Kodachrome" at the top of his lungs. I laughed and sang along with him. Since we were the only ones in sight we both reveled in the lighthearted mood until the moment he pulled out his water bottle and started spraying precious water at me across the hot, dry road. The mood changed dramatically as I reminded him where we were—cycling through the desert in a drought.

South Dakota. We crossed into our sixth state, South Dakota, and the Black Hills National Forest. Low, rocky hills shaded with thick Ponderosa pine forests transformed the desert into gently rolling mountains at South Dakota's highest point. Our ascent was gradual and the peaks appeared rounded and smoothed from centuries of wind and water erosion. We found Jewel Cave National Monument and decided to take a detour to investigate a different kind of landform. Prospectors discovered the caves in 1900, when they were surprised by air rushing out of a natural opening in the rock.

Beautiful formations of cave calcites, limestone, and manganese shone in brilliant crystalline colors of purple, yellows, reds, and gray sparkles. The temperature stayed at a steady 47 degrees as our tour took us down almost 400 feet. We explored for awhile, learned it was a "dry" cave, so we did not see stalactites or stalagmites often found in caves with dripping water. After an hour underground, Paul and I agreed we preferred exploring more on the surface, with our bikes. We camped that night in a comfortable forested campground and watched as the setting sun sent sharp rays through pine boughs, glancing off the dark, tree-covered hills all around us.

Journal Entry ~ August 20, 1974 We enjoyed seeing the Black Hills and are ready to explore more of South Dakota. We're at around 5400' elevation and very much enjoying these roller-coaster hills—fast ups and fast downs, so fun on the bikes. I talked to two young girls traveling by car from British Columbia, and then met up again with the artist Paul had photographed in the Tetons. He recognized me first. He's made a full circle, on his way back to Indiana with photo slides, impressions, and sketches for more interpretive paintings once he gets home. We're very near the middle of our trip, but somehow it seems like most of our hard work is behind us. Flat lands, smaller states and our imaginations have us pushing full speed ahead. We won't ever run out of things to see. And we still have 1800 miles to go!

Stone Monuments. Sections of the Black Hills display bare solid granite that seem to attract artistic souls who can imagine shapes in the rock face. In Custer we found directions to the Crazy Horse Monument. I was anxious to investigate this earthwork I had heard about. The project on Thunderhead Mountain was started as a one-man endeavor by 70-year-old Korczak Ziolkowski. In 1948 he planned a tribute to Native nations and to Chief Crazy Horse, an Oglala war chief. The finished sculpture was designed to stand 500 feet tall and depict Crazy Horse riding his brave steed. The initial stage involved rough blasting away tons of rock and we could see the head and outstretched arm beginning to take shape.

The museum was also Ziolkowski's home, and there we learned about the energy and determination of this man. He had been an assistant working on the Mt. Rushmore project and in 1939 he received a request from Chief Henry Standing Bear: "My fellow chiefs and I would like the white man to know that the red men had great heroes also." The sculptor apparently began construction on his own, climbing up a hand-built stairway to chip rocks away, even before a road could be built for larger equipment. Back in Custer, though, the local population seemed a bit disconcerted about the project. We were unable to find photos or even much information about Crazy Horse Monument. The tour guide told us that it was not being well-received in the town, and there was a lack of respect for the native population there. While at Crazy Horse we heard of friction between locals and the workers on the mountain. So far, no government help or financial assistance supported the project. While traveling through South Dakota we noticed varying reactions and information from a lot of different viewpoints about the endeavor.

In the Black Hills we entered a completely different world, away from flat plains and surrounded by wind-smoothed shapes and surfaces. The sky was crystal blue; granite and pines against the vivid backdrop brought the scenery alive with contrasting textures. Nature surely had been at work creating art and incomparable beauty. As we stopped to admire some impressive rock outcroppings and pillars, Paul suddenly pointed up to the ridge. Behind one of the natural stone walls, out peeked a familiar profile, we were viewing the back of Mt. Rushmore.

Laughing, he called out,

"Oh, Hi, George, almost didn't see you there!"

The great stonework on the side of that mountain was impressive. Gutzon Borglum worked with 30 engineers and modern equipment to carve four 60-foot heads between 1927 and 1941. Each face was meant to express one of the ideals symbolic of this nation: Washington represents Independence; Jefferson speaks for Self-Government; Lincoln for Permanence; and Roosevelt for Political Economics. Patriotic music was piped in around the museum grounds and viewers learned about the history and details of the creation of the monument. Puffy popcorn clouds drifted above and across the valley beyond the imposing stone heads of the Presidents. It brought to mind the vast country we'd been riding across but then, we remembered how many miles we'd need to cover before nightfall.

A family from Kansas had been at both of the monuments at the same time we were, and at Rushmore they stopped to inquire about our trip. They asked us to pose in front of our bicycles for a picture to add to their album. We were to be a part of their trip across the country, and we were a little thrilled at the thought of the family we'd just met taking a record of our journey home with them.

Coasting at top speed down the steep grade from Mt. Rushmore on our way out of the Black Hills, Paul almost ran into the back of a travel-trailer. The bulk and weight of the trailer navigating the curves must have made the driver uneasy. As we coasted around the corner, picking up speed on the narrow road, he suddenly slowed down right in front of us as he braked for the curve. Paul got tight on his tail and let the width of the vehicle break the wind, riding the slipstream right behind the guy for a half-mile downhill. I could see the blinking brake lights and was afraid Paul was following too closely. The trailer was going too slow for us, we could not pass him on the curves. Frustrated, we finally pulled over to wait until he was far ahead.

Photo-worthy scenery slowed us down so it took a couple of days to leave the striking landscape behind, a nice break from the monotony of the high desert plains. We spent those couple of days appreciating the woods and cool shade of picnic areas. Paul pulled off at every vista point, perching on top of a rock or hillock looking out across rolling green hills to capture the broad view through the wide-angle lens of his camera. We continued to enjoy the short climbs and quick downhill coasts and lots of freewheeling, easy riding.

Rapid City. Taking advantage of city services in Rapid City, we stayed over to catch up and gather supplies we had been missing in the small towns and one-store hamlets. We made stops at a camera store, the bike shop, a bank, an optometrist to repair sunglasses, and the supermarket. We took time to explore a museum and had a brief detour to see a historic wooden Norwegian church. We gorged ourselves at a McDonald's, Shakey's Pizza Parlor, and we fit all that in after a sweet-filled breakfast at Ray's Bakery. Not that we were starving for civilization and junk food. The city had me missing the wild open spaces, and Paul agreed. During our visit I was nearly run over at an intersection, we got lost in the middle of town, and we paid ridiculous prices for two nights camping at an uncomfortable trailer-camper parking lot.

We were finding it easier to meet people now that we had more traveling experience. Occasionally we'd be in a store or stopped at a gas station and someone would ask, "You from California?"

Paul and I would exchange glances, thinking *why is this so obvious?* Then one of us would answer: "Yes, how did you know?"

"Oh, we get a lot of them from out there," one man commented as he took our money for snacks.

Then a typical response came from another local resident, "Mostly people around here wouldn't think of riding a bike across the country."

An older gentleman at the Rapid City trailer park spoke with us in a thick German accent. He was really curious about our trip and eventually confessed that he had toured the Mediterranean countries on a bike in 1932, when he was 21. His bulky frame shook all over when he laughed, recalling some of his favorite memories. He said he had traveled with a friend on balloon-tire bikes that weighed 93 pounds with gear stuffed in packs and baskets. He was currently on a bus tour with some other German travelers, but their bus had broken down and they were waiting for parts. Although he enjoyed seeing the sights on this trip, he assured us that the best time of his life had been on that bicycle ride over 40 years ago. We could relate!

A guy and a girl came into a lunch counter while we were eating, looking as shredded and worn as we felt, weathered skin and tattered clothing. They had just completed a thousand-mile walk in the Canadian Yukon. We invited them to sit with us and they overflowed with tales of their experiences—hiking for two weeks at a time in wet boots carrying everything they needed with them. They followed roads, trails, wagon roads, and even cow paths. The guy said it was really easy to get lost, but somehow they always found themselves headed the right way. That day they were hitchhiking back to Michigan where he would soon start a job as an art teacher. Their summer walk sounded like quite an adventure, reminding us were not alone in our journey of discovery.

The interstate leaving Rapid City was narrow and hectic with traffic, which made for uncomfortable riding, so we explored some side roads until we found a quiet ranch access road that took us through tiny towns and open fields of agricultural land dotted with farm buildings. Corn and wheat were in abundance and we noticed the farmers were irrigating great swaths of land. The road was deserted all day and the going was much easier. The wind was up, blowing straight out of the South, howling with all its might, gathering strength over miles and miles of uninterrupted prairie. The sky was clear, my mind was open; I rode the pedals rhythmically, unencumbered along this uncluttered section of countryside. The feeling of freedom was uplifting, like nothing else I had experienced.

Wasta Railroad Depot. After another 37 miles we found another remarkable small town off the main road. At first it was difficult to find, hidden around the corner in a narrow river valley once we dropped down into a low spot. We wanted to get some coffee and catch a short rest. Thunderheads were gathering over the distant Black Hills, and I wasn't in the mood for riding in the rain, so we decided to stay. There were probably 500 residents but Wasta, incredibly, had two campgrounds. We found Bruce's Campground and were the sole campers that night. The attendant was very friendly and gave us some history of the area. She told us the main resource in the town was their sweet spring water and the railroad that had once brought life to Wasta.

"These days," she said, "one train comes through twice a day and it rarely stops. The old depot is sadly neglected and nearly deserted now."

Back in Blackfoot, Idaho, Paul and I had been impressed by a renovated train depot that someone had converted into a home, complete with a red caboose studio. We wandered over to the Wasta station to investigate. It was indeed dilapidated, a run-down, two-story wood-slatted building that had been ransacked and abandoned.

Searching through the debris and piles of trash we found two porcelain doorknobs and a metal spike from the tracks. It didn't seem like they would be missed, so we decided to collect these treasures and carry them till we could ship them home. I imagined they might one day be installed in our own studio, maybe in a caboose.

Prairie dogs popped into view on the way out of Wasta—we'd found the prairie dog town our hostess had described to us. The furry rodent-like animals built mounds all over the place where they sat up straight out of their holes and kept an eye on whatever was happening. They were fascinating to watch, but soon we left those little guys behind and started noticing wooden signs and billboards cluttering the roadside proclaiming the wonders of Wall Drug. As we approached, what seemed like hundreds of signs appeared, with increasingly crazy slogans:

COME TO WALL, S.D.— HOME OF WALL DRUG
FREE WATER AT WALL DRUG
DON'T MISS WALL DRUG
HAVE YOU DUG WALL DRUG?
and finally, the best play on words:
WALL, WE'RE GLAD YOU MADE IT!

The town sat at the edge of the Badlands of South Dakota, and apparently the name "Wall" came from a natural earthen wall or ledge leading into the area. As soon as we pulled onto the main street, we saw that the tourist spot was rocking with motorcycles, camper trailers, and people milling about on every corner enjoying ice cream cones and all the free ice water they could gulp down. We had a drink, had a laugh, and continued on our journey through hot, dusty South Dakota. Not far out of Wall, we spotted another herd of pronghorn antelope. They seemed perfectly suited to their environment and I could almost feel the joyful spring in their gait as I watched them running and leaping in the distance.

Journal Entry ~ August 24, 1974 So far in South Dakota we have been feeling the water shortage. There has been a marked lack of shower facilities and when there is something available there's always an extra charge. It's been five days since we washed up and we are in a rest area with a 3-foot high green metal water pipe sticking out of the dirt. So we just stood out in the field, both in our shortest shorts and me in my bikini top, scrubbing up with a bandana washrag. It felt soooo good to let the dust and grime drip away as clean, cool water evaporated from my skin. I was even tempted to do my hair, but we should hopefully find warm water in Pierre tomorrow. It's good to have a helpful spouse around to pump the water while you bathe out on the prairie.

Pierre. After crossing the wide Missouri River we slowed down just outside a hotel in Pierre. We were deciding whether to spend money for a room since we were in the capital city when two youngsters on sting-rays approached us, all blue eyed and blond haired.

"You guys just traveling through? Have you ridden very far on those bikes?" the older one, around 11, asked.

"Yes, we've ridden from California. Know where that is?"

He proudly announced that he knew all about California from geography lessons. Then I asked, "Have you lived in Pierre all your life?"

"Yep. It's pronounced *Peer.* It's a nice town, you know, it's the capital. Smallest capital in the country, and right in the middle of the United States. The center of the country is right around here you know. It's a good town, and pretty well located, too!"

"Do you know if we'd be able to camp in a park in town?" I asked.

"I got a better place than that for you to go." He was outgoing and confident.

Paul and I were cracking up at this little guy's enthusiasm, but we listened intently. He told us his friend's father owned the best motel in town. He said if we go there, and tell them he sent us, we should ask for the best room. Of course we could not pass up this glowing recommendation, so we checked in at his friend's place. It was a bit pricier than we usually spent, and we probably didn't actually get the best room, but it was a good place to stay. We had air conditioning, a television, a real shower, and fresh white sheets to sleep in that night. After a late snack from a restaurant across the street we stayed up too late watching movies.

Next morning we listened to the guy who ran the motel as he explained how he happened to have a clock hanging in his office that was from J.D. Rockefeller III's private railroad car. The tale involved rattlesnakes, a career choice, and a few pointed compliments on my tan. We made a stop at the post office to pick up mail at General Delivery. Then we looked for a bike store to replace some of our lost tools and a new saddle for Paul's bike.

Pat Springer and his dad ran a very cool shop in the cellar of their home called the Cycle Cellar. We admired his custom shiny silver bike and found out he was the president of the local bike club. They kept a notebook in the shop where bicycle tourers could leave signatures and notes about where they had been as they passed through town. We flipped the pages and recognized a couple of riders we had met the week before in Wyoming. We signed in, wrote some notes, and promised to send a postcard from the East Coast to add to their collection. Pierre had left us in good spirits after meeting so many interesting characters, so we hung out that day exploring and in the late afternoon got a spot in a rest area outside of town to camp for the night.

Native Americans. We were just looking around for the flattest spot to settle into when three people came up to us and asked if it was okay to camp there. We said sure, and they set up right next to us. After dinner, we talked for awhile about their travels.

They were members of the Menomonee tribe from Wisconsin. Driving a decorated VW bus, they told us they worked the pow-wow circuit and described it as kind of like a carnival but based more on the traditions and folklore of their people. One of the young men told me he was a dancer. Then he showed me some beautiful handmade silver and turquoise jewelry he and his wife would be selling at the pow-wow. He said he owned a jewelry store in Milwaukee. As they pitched their large tent his friend came out of the van carrying a feathered staff with a stand. He explained it was their national flag, made up of 13 red and white eagle feathers. He showed me his wide brimmed leather hat that sported a single eagle feather he had received from his father, a chief of their tribe. The woman did not speak with us that evening. She smiled at us and kept busy arranging their campsite.

I was curious and wanted to spend some time talking with the more outgoing man to learn more about the life he lived, especially after we had been learning about historical events and conflicts between Native peoples and settlers as we traveled. We sat side by side on the ground and I listened while he spoke softly, thoughtfully, about their plight.

He said he had broken away from the reservation where he had been raised and could not go back. He tried to describe how his citizenship wasn't the same as what he called a "free American," and that all native-owned businesses, including his jewelry store, were tightly controlled by the Bureau of Indian Affairs. He sounded frustrated because he was attempting to push past the oppression he had experienced by going into business on his own, but he struggled because there was no encouragement from the government or even from his own people. He said he sensed a kind of jealousy between tribal members whenever one strikes out to become successful, and perhaps find more prosperity than his brothers. That, he said, was a contradiction to the Menomonee way of submission, as he called it. Many of his people instead refused to involve themselves in anything but the simple, poor life they had on the reservation.

When I mentioned we had visited the site of the Crazy Horse monument, he told me he was a personal friend to the sculptor Ziolkowski. He had heard rumors circulating that the man was simply trying to take advantage of local businesses and didn't actually work on the Crazy Horse carving. But he said he knew that the project was a serious undertaking and that Ziolkowski enlisted only Native people to help work on the sculpture. He felt certain that the monument would be completed.

We didn't get their names, and rainy weather prevented us from getting pictures in the morning. But it was enriching to have met them and to hear firsthand about their experiences and struggles. There was much that I did not understand, and I thought a lot about our conversation as we headed out on our bikes.

Little House On the Prairie. One more relatively big town on this long, straight highway was Huron. As we neared the edge of town, a traffic cop stopped and waved us over to his vehicle with a polite warning for us to ride carefully. The state fair was happening that weekend and he said crowds were driving in from all over.

"Be careful, stay well over to the side of the road," he told us.

"You bet," I answered. We were pretty aware of how vulnerable we were on the bikes, always more cautious as we got into traffic situations and populated areas, even in South Dakota. Thankfully, no one had ridden us off the road. Not *yet*, anyway. We noticed people from all over the countryside headed for the fair. People towed trailers, campers, horse trailers, and a few arrived in car clubs. By the time we came into Huron we'd ridden 50 miles, rain was threatening, and we checked around for a place to camp. We found a grassy park on the far side of town set aside for camping and settled in for the night, no energy left for exploring the fair.

Halfway through the following day we rode through DeSmet, a quiet, peaceful place that was the setting for Laura Ingalls Wilder's children's book series, "Little House on the Prairie." She created the stories when she was 60 years old, recounting childhood memories of growing up in a tiny cabin with her family. Full of adventures and hardships, the books described the fun of harvest times, the chilling winters, and the joys of family. I could picture the small town as it had been in the 1870s and '80s, a hundred years ago. We saw plaques on the general store and the first meeting house that had stood during that time. We found a bakery and stuffed ourselves with warm, moist cinnamon rolls, a couple of chocolate frosted old-fashioned donuts and coffee, wondering what it would have been like to survive during those early years of settlement.

Meeting people each day was raising our trip to a new level—where it began as a physical challenge, riding cross-country on bicycles was really broadening my understanding of the people who made up the country. We'd ride all day long through miles and miles of farmland and open fields. We often passed by herds of cattle. Cows grazing along the fence lines were usually quite curious and raised their bulky heads, turned their furry faces, and watched us until we waved or were out of sight. But we were always happy for the chance to meet and talk with interesting people in this sparsely populated area. We encountered so many varied personalities, listened to stories from some truly unique characters, and they always spoke of their love for the land, pride in their heritage and the towns they were part of. I had seen a display in a museum in Pierre that began to make more sense as I noticed replicas of handbills hung in a post office or saloon in these smaller communities.

The Homestead Act of 1862
"South Dakota is now one of the United States. And Her future is assured.
The Undersigned, having control of 100,000 acres of the choicest land
in the Counties of Hughes, Hyde, Potter, and Sully and desiring to afford
home-seekers opportunity to make
personal examination of lands, have arranged for free personally conducted
Excursions by Special Trains, by the C&NW Railway to Pierre, Dakota, Leaving
from Chicago."

Parcels of perhaps 80 or 160 acres of land could be claimed after several years of residence and lots of work and became the legal property of the determined pioneers. These lands were settled by hard-working, dedicated homesteaders, leaving a legacy for all the people we were meeting as we traveled through the plains.

One-Speed Memories. Further down the road Paul and I stopped at a coffee shop and ended up speaking with a gentleman from the tiny town of Wassington. He sat down and asked where we were headed. He said he had lived there all his life, and when he was 16 he got himself a one-speed bike. After doing his chores on the farm he rode 15 miles a day round trip to visit his sweetheart. Rain or shine all year he would ride his bike to see her. Then, 50 years later, there he was describing their life as an old married couple, but he still remembered all those bike rides. He grinned and wished us good luck on our bike ride. We slowed down at a farm later that same day to check out bushel barrels full of apples at a fruit stand outside a huge, whitewashed barn. The farmer happily gave us a tour of his apple orchard, let us sample the juicy fruit right off the trees, and gave us a supply of fresh apples that lasted us a week.

Journal Entry ~ August 30 1974 We crossed the 100th Meridian yesterday, called "The Eastern Edge of the Great American Desert." Really good riding today, we made it further than we planned with wind behind us all day long. Between towns we're watching how terrain changes and where the clouds move across the huge blue dome of the sky. We stopped to watch the corn grow and wondered at how the farmers can stack hay bales taller than buildings. Speeding along effortlessly in 10th gear, pushing mile after mile on the flat, straight road with a perfect tailwind we flew 88 miles into camp, across the border out of South Dakota and into Minnesota. Our longest day so far! Feels like we're getting closer every day.

9  Looking Back ~ Moving Forward

2024 Reflections

Push off and straighten onto the saddle. Regular cadence, rhythmic downstroke, pull up for power. Legs make circles, pedals turn, wheels spin, and I settle into the flow of the ride. Arms, legs, biceps, and quads meld with the bike. Steering is a look, a lean, and a glide into the curve. Lift and speed at the top of a hill creates weightlessness. Body and bicycle geometry perfectly matched.

Air glances off the skin, floating through hairs on my arms, legs, and cheeks. Breezes push scents deeper into lungs and nostrils. Smells intensify. Cool shade, warmer air, currents fall down through hidden small canyons, up a gully, floating off fields of grass. Brown smells different from green, flowering vegetation infuses the air with depth and nuance. Time and distance dissolve into illusion from the seat of my bike. There's an intimate connection with something bigger than myself, being fully in the moment.

Riding in 1974 to Riding at 75. As I write this, I am looking forward to celebrating my 75th birthday, as well as the 50th anniversary of our transcontinental bike ride. We're living in the 70s of our lives and our priorities have changed, but we have not changed in what we see and appreciate of this world. Having ridden a bike for more than half my life, I feel the same effects when I ride the e-bike as when I first got on a bike when I was young.

We are retired in northern Arizona, in the midst of volcanic fields of the San Francisco Peaks and not too far from the high desert and red rock canyons, within a stone's throw of a dozen national parks and monuments. In summer and fall, I'll cruise through different areas of my neighborhood; sometimes it's just around the block. Occasionally we'll explore together, tackling an off-road section of the Arizona Trail.

As soon as we realized we could ride together once again after the years of raising the children, Paul and I set off every summer, reviving in short spurts the thrill of doing a longer ride outside of our daily routine. The first, of course, was the 50-mile ride when I turned 50—the California Coast ride that took us from Morro Bay to the base of Big Sur and the Piedras Blancas Lighthouse. We were able to accomplish that ride a few more summers—each time reviving my love for riding along the Pacific Ocean.

Hawaii, Death Valley. Around our twenty-fifth wedding anniversary, Paul received a bit of extra money from his aunt and he surprised me with airline tickets to visit the island of Maui. Before we left, we located a tour company that rented bicycles. They transported us to the top of Haleakala volcano and sent us off on another downhill ride of a lifetime from the 10,000-foot summit, all the way to the bottom where the road came to an end at the crystal blue ocean. Later that night we drove to the top and watched the sun set on one side while the moon rose on the opposite side of the island.

Then, the year after, to satisfy Paul's love of deserted open spaces, we signed up for the Death Valley Full Moon Century. It was a challenge for me, a dream come true for him. We started the ride together around 5 p.m., but I knew I wouldn't finish. We left the park visitor center with the group, but turned around half-way so that I could get back to the car before I completely passed out. I do remember Paul riding alongside me in the dark as we finished the last uphill bit, he was singing show tunes, carrying my helmet, and making sure I made it safely to the car. He finished the 65-mile metric century by midnight, while I slept, exhausted and peaceful after my 35-mile effort.

Bike Commuting. I finished my college degree while working as an editor at a major publishing company. The office was located in San Fernando Valley, about 15 miles from where we lived in Simi Valley, California. Sitting in traffic during my commute one morning I suddenly realized that I could be riding my bicycle faster than cars were going. That was enough of an incentive. I calculated the miles to a convenient public parking lot just over the hill between those two valleys. A fitness club in the building across from my office had showers and lockers. Until we retired, I bicycled 8 miles twice a day, saved on gas and time, and had my daily dose of exercise doing my favorite thing.

It didn't take long for us to accumulate more bikes than cars once we rekindled our cycling lifestyle. After completing a few group rides along the coast on road bikes, we bought a beautiful pearly white cloud-colored tandem. Then Paul found a sturdy mountain bike that was a bit big for me, which I soon replaced with my lighter, faster Bianchi road bike. Other bikes included a recumbent for him; two new mountain bikes for when we moved to Arizona; and eventually we both fell in love with our Specialized e-bikes. Today we have one hybrid electric Honda automobile and four bicycles in our garage.

Since our retirement home is just an hour's drive from the Grand Canyon, we can carry our bikes on the back of our car to ride along the Rim Trail from Grand Canyon Village to Hermit's Rest. The 16 mile round-trip comes with the most spectacular views so we make it a whole day's adventure. In 2014, Paul successfully completed a 75-mile off-road challenge, riding from Flagstaff to the Grand Canyon while helping raise money for Toys for Tots.

Petrified Forest Ride. Several years ago we discovered another beautiful ride sponsored by Northland Pioneer College as a fundraiser for scholarships, that takes place in the Petrified Forest through the Painted Desert. We've done that Pedal the Petrified ride on road bikes, mountain bikes, Paul's recumbent one year, and most recently on e-bikes. With the extra boost from pedal-assist, we completed the 70 miles pedaling side by side, still our favorite style of riding.

Riding Through the Years. These days, during every ride I am conscious that the climate is not the same. I see change in the rhythms of seasons, the amount of rain and snow falling to feed plants and trees. Temperature extremes affect the number of days I can ride comfortably—in summer the increased UV rays drain away my energy and burn through the sun block after a short time. Winter comes later and I spend more time riding indoors on the trainer, even when there's no snow.

I'm just coming back after a 30 minute ride on this 50-degree day in February. I am energized, happy to stretch out the legs after a brief and weak snowfall yesterday. It's already melted. By now we'd normally have two-foot snow drifts piled against the north side of the house. We are all adjusting to the changes in climate, the unpredictability of weather patterns around the globe. It informs my day-to-day decisions about what the day's exercise or workout is going to be, what I should wear outdoors, when I can plant flowers and start the vegetable garden. I find consistency in what I feel when I ride—the physical nature of riding a bike is the same whether it's on a mountain bike, a road bike, or my e-bike.

Long before I could grasp any of these heady life lessons, however, we had to figure out how to get ourselves out of the Plains states and all the way to the East Coast.

10 MIDWEST to EAST COAST

Minnesota . Wisconsin . Michigan . Canada . New York

The Upper Midwest states include Minnesota, Wisconsin, and Michigan, and we crossed through the narrow northern sections of these three states as summer's mild weather was showing signs of autumn. We immediately noticed the changes in the terrain. Waterways and river valleys flowed between rolling hills carved by ancient glaciers shaping the land, leaving behind unique features. Minnesota is known as "The Land of 10,000 Lakes," and the five Great Lakes define the northern sections we rode. Within the first hours across the border we spotted two small lakes and being near water brightened my mood. At the same time, I considered how the pioneers faced unknown territories at this point in their westward journey. This was where they encountered unfamiliar lands—the desolate landscape we were just riding away from as we navigated through greener areas and more populated towns and cities. We were unfamiliar with midwestern ways and were about to come up against a couple of uncomfortable experiences.

Our 3000-Mile Milestone. "Hey, Paul, it should be right about here, don't you think?" We were moving fast along a deserted section of Highway 14 and I was shouting into a headwind. "We just passed that sign saying we're 5 miles from Lamberton. Want to make it a celebration?"

"Can you imagine that?" Paul called back as he slowed his bike. "I wonder if folks back home will believe it? 3,000 miles! We've really done it! And we pedaled every mile on these two ten-speeds!"

I opened my journal to a blank page and scribbled big blocky numbers: **3-0-0-0-!** Then I posed standing right in the middle of the road while Paul got the picture to prove it. The feeling was awesome, indescribable; swelling with pride and accomplished and yet, it was just another mile on our journey. We had met one guy back in Oregon who had 10,000 miles of touring to his credit. This moment was *ours*. We'd been enjoying ourselves every minute of the months we'd been traveling. June 9 to August 31. I tried to picture all those miles between where we stood and where we had started—it blew my mind. I started to form a tangible impression of the distance we'd covered as I thought back: South Dakota, Wyoming, Idaho, Washington, Oregon, California—what a long, strange trip indeed.

We rode on through Minnesota that afternoon gazing across cornfields and soybean plantations that seemed to go on forever, punctuated by lots of little towns cropping up every 10 miles or so. Old farm communities full of beautiful old buildings in a style more eastern and solid-looking than we had seen on the prairie. There were lots of opportunities for us to take breaks and Paul was delighted to find so many bakeries. We stopped in a little place called Sleepy Eye to admire a decorative two-tone brick building on the corner with brightly-colored glass windows and found a pastry shop for a welcome treat.

Township Names. After Sleepy Eye, we began an entertaining game. We were having trouble making sense of our destinations since all the little spots sounded so similar. We challenged each other to come up with a single characteristic name for a Midwestern town based on what we were seeing on the map and on road signs. So many places seemed to carry a suffix following a particular land feature: ...ton, ...man, ... field, ...ville, the convention was unfamiliar to us. So what sounded better: Lakeville, Waterton, or maybe Smithtonfieldville? Mind games like this kept us occupied as we ticked off the miles in this new landscape.

The map showed a perfectly straight line all the way to New Ulm. It was a surprise to be so far into Minnesota on the first afternoon. We had been averaging 50 to 70 miles a day, depending on the road conditions, the weather, and our moods. That day a storm was building behind us and wind pushed us onward at a quick pace. There's nothing like flying down the road with the gift of a strong tailwind. Nature seemed to be saying "Yes, yes, go for 100 miles—halfway across a state in one day!" But then, I felt the familiar pangs of hunger. Our appetites had doubled and tripled since we were riding hard all day.

As we coasted through the next town we fell victim to the A&W stand so we slowed down. We sat resting and sipping sweet root beers, letting the stormy weather catch up with us. That afternoon we only covered 15 miles before deciding to camp in the next town park. A sign offered free space for "Bonified Campers Only." We celebrated with a dinner of packaged spaghetti in honor of our 3,000-mile milestone. Paul found two strong, sturdy trees good for pitching the tent and we settled down with hot tea until sleepiness overtook us. The next morning my legs reminded me of the previous day's long ride, close to 90 miles, and it took some loosening up before I could mount up and ride again.

On the long stretches of roads, I noted for the first time that our natural pace and cadences differed. Paul seemed to be going twice as fast as me, his bike covered more ground with each stroke so he was always gaining on me. I either had to pedal faster or he had to slow down and wait for me, but we worked it out and enjoyed occasionally riding solitary through the gentle countryside. I suspected that he was becoming more focused on the goal ahead, while I was more distracted, checking out the different types of corn growing, admiring the tall slender silos, and chatting with cows hanging out along the fenced roadside. We talked with residents wherever we stopped, and people in cars waved or tooted horns more often than we had experienced along the roads in less populated states.

Journal Entry ~ September 1, 1974 *We're huddled inside the tent early tonight at Shields Lake in this campground packed full for Labor Day. On the large map up we had on the wall at home we had scheduled to be near Minneapolis today. We're just below it so, looks like we're keeping up with our plan. We've had a few cold nights and chilly mornings, and as the thermometer drops we tend to want to cover more ground. Hopefully we'll be at Paul's folks' before weather turns too cold to ride. I've been having some cramps and it's uncomfortable, especially when I'm feeling the cold all over. Traveling with my patient husband is very precious when I don't feel great. Maybe he doesn't quite know what it feels like on days like this, but he is always kind and tries to make me feel better—smiling and ready with a soft touch or a wildflower to tuck into my hair.*

Mississippi River. Finally we reached Red Wing, Minnesota, riding the Great River Road along the banks of the Mississippi River. We stayed in the historic red brick St. James Hotel and checked out our room: 12-foot ceilings, a great old footed bathtub, and a window overlooking the wide Mississippi. Our bikes had to stay downstairs in the storage room, but the bed was soft and sleeping on clean sheets was quite comfortable. We rather missed our regular camping routine, but we found out later the temperature had dropped to freezing overnight, so stopping at the hotel was a good decision.

We took time out the next day to give the bikes some much needed attention. We borrowed a couple of rags from the hotel and went to work on layer after layer of dirt and grease caked onto the frames and chains. Scraping, cleaning, and re-oiling really made a difference. The bikes had certainly been good to us all these miles. My air pump and kickstand had disappeared somewhere along the way but losing those items didn't make much difference so we carried on.

Invention of Zipper Pants. In the hotel room I noticed I finally had worn too many holes in my jeans shorts and decided to make myself some convertible shorts/pants to match Paul's. Before we left Santa Barbara, he had come up with an idea to cut the legs off a pair of his long blue jeans, make a hem for shorts, and sew zippers onto the top and bottom pieces. He could ride in long pants in the mornings and then, as the day warmed up, it was ultra-convenient to just unzip and pull off the long leg parts without having to change clothes by the side of the road. We located a good deal on a pair of rugged boy's pants for $1.97 at the General Store. I bought two zippers, thread, and a tough needle in the same store, and took advantage of the second night at the hotel to stitch them up by hand. The only tricky part was making sure I set both sides of the zippers going the same direction in a way that I could reach the tabs easily. They fit me perfectly and were quite welcome since the weather had started to turn colder. It was a bit emotional throwing out the cutoffs I had worn all those miles but made sense to shed an extra piece of gear.

Next day, taking the bicycles across the slow moving Mississippi I recalled so many stories of that mighty river—Mark Twain's novels, rhythm and blues tunes, and movie scenes depicting the Big Muddy. To me it had always signified a line marking western and eastern sections of the country. Crossing that legendary waterway on bikes meant that we were getting closer to the end of our journey. The Red Wing Bridge, also known as the Dwight D. Eisenhower Bridge, took us across the state line and we arrived in Wisconsin. Another state to explore!

Wisconsin. Rest areas in the new state immediately won our five-star rating and we enjoyed the greenery and grassy spots to settle for lunch. We were making good progress, but already I was noticing evidence of approaching autumn. Colors of red and gold tinged a few leaves overhead, sometimes only a branch or two, but the urgency to make miles was strong. Our plan was to ride through the state to the ferry that would take us across Lake Michigan. We did take time to notice the cornfields were noisy with cracking-popping sounds as the stalks stretched taller and the deep green fronds held huge cobs that were close to ripening. We tasted famous Wisconsin cheese, thinly sliced right from the processor. It was fresh and delicious, and spiced up our lunches.

Our stop in Neillsville was rather unfortunate. As soon as we hit town we looked for the chief of police, as usual, to find out about stopping in the park overnight. He wasn't in his office, apparently he was making his rounds, because we spotted his vehicle driving around the next block. We headed back to the Town Hall to wait. A few minutes later, we found out that he had had a heart attack and died while we were sitting in his office.

I still needed to ask someone about camping out, so I found two men talking in the doorway of one of the offices.

"Excuse me, I am so sorry to interrupt. Do you know if it would be okay for us to camp out in the park here? We're on bicycles and just have a small tent and a propane stove."

Their mood was subdued, a little confused since no one was really in charge right then. They looked at me, then at each other, then one shrugged and said,

"I don't see any problem. Go ahead, it's just down on 1st Street. You shouldn't have any trouble."

I thanked them and quickly left with Paul to retrieve our bikes and find the park. It was pretty big for a small town, with a playground bordered by a small forest.

"I feel weird about being here. I guess we can just pick anywhere over by those trees where we'll be kind of hidden, okay?" Paul said.

"Yeah, I don't know if anybody in town is going to pay attention to us tonight. I feel so bad for his family. What an awful thing to find out about a person dying while we were looking for him. Do you feel like eating?"

"Yeah, kinda. What do we have?" he asked.

"There's this box of macaroni and cheese, want to go for it? It'll taste good and maybe make us feel a little better to have something different. Can you fill the pot with water? It'll take a few minutes to boil and we'll need to wait for the noodles to cook."

He found the faucet by the bathrooms while I set up the tiny camp stove, plugged in the canister, and turned the valve to light the flow of gas. It didn't take long to cook, and I squeezed some extra butter from the squirt bottle to give it a little more flavor. Comfort food.

We settled into the tent, but the night was somber, feeling sad for the man we had never met.

"I'm glad we're just passing through," I spoke quietly. "This is such a small town, I guess it's going to hit everyone hard."

"I know. Hope we can get some sleep tonight." We dozed off pretty quickly after a strange day in another new place.

The townspeople were welcoming enough the next day. We bought a dozen fresh-baked cookies and talked with some of the ladies inside the main street grocery store. We watched some men working in the corn mill and asked them about their process, and later we stopped at a gas station for water and found the manager tending the flowerbed near the pumps. He offered us prayer cards and his good wishes for a safe, successful ride. These brief encounters were special, slices of real life: we had barely a glimpse, a quick flash, or a brief impression of a person's character and then, as we rode on, I tried to imagine more of their story, their personality, what their life must be like. In these moments I was touched by the light of so many different people. I felt warmer inside, then, because we had crossed paths.

Journal Entry ~ September 7, 1974 We slept late again this morning, until 8:30, and got off to a bad start. We had a horrible riding day—the roads were hilly, narrow, bumpy, with no shoulder. Trucks and traffic sped by too fast and too impolite, not sympathetic to bikes on the side of their road. So far this was close to, if not right on, the worst day we've had for riding since we left. The Bighorns was a difficult challenge but this part of the ride has been downright uncomfortable. Hope today is better.

Another work friend had given me contact information for her sister who lived on a farm near Stevens Point, Wisconsin. We phoned them the morning we expected to arrive, but it was a 70-mile day and we didn't get to the little settlement near their place until 8 p.m. where we called from a phone booth. Alex Olden told us to wait there so he could pick us up. We settled the bikes in his truck bed and got a ride right up to the door of a 90-year-old farmhouse sitting on 80 acres of corn, grain, and forests.

Bountiful Harvest. The family spread the harvest table with warmed-over food from their dinner, and we ate until it seemed we were not being polite anymore. Then, as we gathered in the living room, I kept rearranging myself on the floor with the kids, unaccustomed to sitting on an actual couch. Next day was Saturday and they were free from all but a few chores, so we stayed for a leisurely and bountiful farm-style breakfast spread: eggs and fruit, country potatoes, thick slices of fresh bread slathered with homemade strawberry jam, coffee, milk, and juice. The three children, Will, George, and Alice were bursting with enthusiasm and did not want us to leave. Alex and Jean mentioned the possibility of rain, and when they promised Sunday dinner would involve freshly harvested sweet corn there was no way we could turn down the chance to spend another night on their living room floor.

The youngest, Will, hauled out his toy farm trucks to plow the carpet, told us stories, and spilled his little-boy liveliness all over the place. George tried hard to get us to go ride the horses, but when he couldn't convince us to ride live animals he organized a 5-man, 3-Frisbee match out front to expend some of his unbounded energy. Alice practiced being hostess, serving plates of chocolate chip cookies as she shyly asked many questions about our trip, our lives, and our plans. We ate too much, got a look at the alfalfa fields, vegetable garden, two cows, two sheep, and the untouched forest backland surrounding the working section of the farm. The pastoral setting and the pure enjoyment we witnessed visiting this family gave us something to consider about how we might choose a farm life somewhere in our future. When it was time to go, a limp fog had settled over the rolling fields and we were reluctant to leave. The family gathered out in front of the farmhouse to wave goodbye as we pedaled out their long driveway toward our next adventure.

Run Off the Road. Route 10 was a two-lane highway leading straight on to Manitowoc. We figured it would take us two days to get to our ferry crossing. Still on schedule, it seemed like we would arrive in time if we covered 50 miles each of those days. I tried to settle into the rhythm of the road. With too many cars whizzing by, squeezed into a too-narrow shoulder, I kept my focus on the railroad tracks off to my right, paralleling the highway. There was a bit of gravel and then a 20-foot wide strip of weeds and dirt between where I rode and where I hoped a train might rumble by. I was about a half-dozen car-lengths ahead of Paul, daydreaming and watching the tracks, when suddenly I was startled by a truck horn blaring right on top of me. The 18-wheeler's engine roar sounded like Godzilla was creeping up my back.

I barely saw the wall of metal speed by, felt the downdraft shove me and the bike sideways as my arms wavered with shock from the fright, even as my hands instinctively gripped the brakes. I reacted quickly but still couldn't keep the bike steady enough. My skinny tires veered off the road into the gravel. Thankfully, I'd acquired a lot of riding experience and muscle strength, but with the weight of rear packs affecting my momentum, every muscle contracted as I fell sideways without injury.

I hopped back onto the saddle and maneuvered over to the pavement, but I was still badly frightened. Paul was fuming. He rode up beside me quickly, checked that I was okay, protectively moved his front wheel next to my rear tire on the traffic side, and continued the rest of that section hovering right on my tail. The trucker sped off right away; we just kept on moving. It was a good couple of miles before the adrenaline dissipated and I stopped shaking.

We both carried some of that anger for quite a few miles. We'd ridden over 3,000 miles and this was the first really dangerous incident we'd had. The traffic was not the issue; it was just a stupid, thoughtless driver making a statement to scare a bicycle rider. We were sure he passed Paul and took more pleasure in making trouble for a girl rider. After a few miles of riding, I worked out the toxic feelings and calmed down. Thankfully, it didn't take long to get back into the beauty of the ride. One more day and we'd be ferrying across Lake Michigan.

Neena Menasha and the Ferry. Two delightful sister towns nestled in a little river valley by Lake Winnebago, Neenah and Menasha, surprised us with quaint neighborhoods and tree-lined streets. Tidy, brightly painted houses, every one with a covered front porch, lots of playgrounds and parks made for pleasant exploring. We also discovered the industrial feel of the area when we rode past paper mills and spotted a foundry where they manufactured cast iron grates, frames, and manhole covers to be shipped all over the country. We slept at a rest area outside of town only 25 miles from Manitowoc. Crossing Lake Michigan had been a significant target, drawing us forward ever since Yellowstone and the Bighorns. There were donuts to fuel our morning and mail to pick up at the post office. We passed by a submarine displayed at the spot where 15 subs were built during WWII and transported down the Mississippi.

Our timing was perfect to catch the car ferry. The last regular trip for the summer was scheduled that day; we pulled up with just enough time for lunch before the 1:00 boat left. Had we arrived the next day, we would have had to wait around until the shipping company had reason to cross. Our fare with the bikes was pricey—$10.50 each, but worth it to save us bicycling through Chicago. I looked across the water to what appeared to me to be the horizon and realized it was all lake, not the sea. We turned our bikes over to baggage handlers and kept a close eye on them until we were certain our packs and bikes were safely aboard the City of Midland ferry. It was uncomfortable to be separated from the wheels that had essentially become a part of us over the last three months.

Paul got his sea legs right away, having spent time as a sailor aboard an aircraft carrier. He enjoyed walking the decks and exploring, watching the seagulls skim the ferry's wake and soar across the smooth, placid lake surface. The weather was misty and a little foggy, and I settled into a deck chair, hoping for a bit of a nap. The wind came up strong once we were farther out from shore, so I moved inside for the six-mile crossing. We met the crewmen while they were struggling to balance the bikes on the dock at Ludington as we entered our newest state—Michigan.

Michigan. The afternoon was sinking into the misty evening and we were hungry right on schedule. The last few camping days had been a little less than pleasant—no running water for cooking or showers, expensive camp parks had been our only choice. We weren't sure what we'd find at Michigan rest areas or camping spots, so we stopped first at the sheriff's office in Ludington. The duty officer was more than willing to help; he took time to step away from his paper-strewn desk and took a look at our map. He gave us directions to what he thought would be a friendly campground.

Journal Entry ~ September 12, 1974 We did some juggling of routes yesterday, there was a strong south wind and we had to travel south for quite a few miles. We rode down to Route 46 and camped at Six Lakes. Now we'll have a straight eastward run for at least a day. Maple trees have lost some leaves, turning colors—reds and golds veined with green and yellow—our first close-up taste of autumn. Sometimes the trees along the roadside form a long corridor and we're pedaling through a leaf tunnel. The camp was practically empty by this pretty little lake. And...we only have a couple of weeks to go!

We headed north along the lake shore for a few miles, riding along tree-lined streets through neighborhoods of regal looking houses. We passed a cemetery dotted with huge stone monuments and then found our camp under a forest of green leafy maples, dogwoods, and horse chestnut trees. The sheriff was right, we were greeted by the friendly camp host who gave us a special discount for our different mode of transportation. She pointed out which routes through the state would be hilly and where we would find pretty scenery and good riding. We set up our tent in a deserted section of the campground, had free showers, and slept well after spending the day being ferried across the lake.

Lots of water in this land of lakes, the air was humid from all the ponds, rivers, streams, and puddles we passed. We had expected to find more populated areas but found undeveloped land covered with goldenrod, open fields of brush and wild grasses busy with migrating birds. A fishing resort and a variety of shops catered to vacationers and tourists and towns looked more like cities here in comparison to the gas-station-post-office-one-bar towns we had become used to. To avoid interstate connectors, following the advice of the campground host, we plotted a couple of long zig-zags to get across the state to the southern border.

The next day we cruised through more forest and took our first zig south after a quiet night in an empty tourist park. The glacial effects that long ago had left the land full of ridges made riding difficult. Wind blew from the south as soon as we turned south—headwinds were always so frustrating and made for difficult riding. At the first town we came to, we found a road that would take us more easterly, and we thought it might make the riding more pleasant. It worked! The wind let up, we enjoyed seeing a new kind of farmland—not quite as rambling as in Wisconsin or Minnesota. There were no grain silos, but

I was seeing larger, weathered wood barns at every farm, apparently to protect the harvest and livestock. The camp at Six Lakes turned out to be along six blue lakes strung together like a daisy chain, providing a pleasant afternoon of rest and the camping by water was a welcome comfort.

Tornado at the Honey Bee Festival. Saginaw was along the main road, but we chose to avoid another city as we continued along on alternate roads leading south and east, then south again and east, making miles in the right direction along quiet country roads. Eventually we rode into Chesaning, a small place full of nice quiet neighborhoods. Downtown was blocked off for the Honey Bee Festival—a carnival, a parade, and the main event: crowning of the Honey Bee Queen. A patrolman gave us directions to the town park where people would be camping from all around the county. I was thrilled to have arrived at another festival.

There was always an air of excitement when we came to a place where all the residents were celebrating. Paul found me a balloon to play with, and we were in a jovial mood as we started to empty packs and set up for the evening. We ate, washed up the pots, and went off to explore the rest of the park and festivities. Suddenly, emergency sirens and truck horns went off all around the camp. It looked like something tragic had happened and I hoped no one was seriously injured or ill, especially after the death of that sheriff in Wisconsin. We noticed the patrolman who had directed us to the park was heading right for us.

"You two had better head back into town. They've spotted a tornado coming this way and we've got about a half hour." He spoke slowly, but with a tone of serious urgency.

"You mean there's an actual tornado, coming this way, into the park?" I gasped.

"Well, ma'am, it's sure possible. But we don't want to wait around to find out!" he answered.

"Really!" I was confused, neither of us knew exactly what we should do next.

The sheriff noted our hesitancy and inexperience and offered his assistance. "If you want to ride up in the patrol car and leave your bikes here you can get to safety faster."

Paul stepped in. "No, we'll make it all right riding."

We scurried back to the campsite and grabbed the bikes, slamming everything together and looping the bungees over our stuff. At least we hadn't pitched the tent. My mind was spinning: *Will we make it in time? Is everything attached? What did I forget? What makes it safer in town with all the people crowding together?* It didn't make any sense. This was nothing like a California earthquake. We had a warning, but we had no idea how to get to safety.

Once we were on the main street, walking the bikes and weaving between families and strangers, we noticed the majority of people were heading into brick buildings marked with yellow air-raid or fallout shelter symbols—remnants of wartime. For a suspenseful 45 minutes we wandered around with a couple hundred other frantic citizens. My instinct, along with Paul's, was the same. We wanted to leave the congested area and try to fend for ourselves, but of course with no experience in tornado country, we followed along trying to figure out what to do. A few hysterical women on front porches were yelling to passers-by that everyone was about to be killed. Chamber of Commerce volunteers were calmly ushering people into the basement shelters. The majority of people were calm, ordering coffees and Cokes from the drugstore soda fountain, most of them staring at me and Paul and our fully loaded bicycles.

The Honey Bee Festival only suffered from emotional disruption that evening, but no tornado damage. Thankfully, the storm drove it farther north toward Saginaw where it left little serious damage. I sighed with relief, a little let down and exhausted after all the excitement. I couldn't help but think, *What if a tornado had touched down there? What if the patrolman had forgotten there were bike tourers somewhere in a corner of the park?* Enough what-ifs, I slept well despite the dry, haunting wind that blew through town and rattled our tent that night.

More Michigan Impressions. The next day we hurried through Montrose, Otisville, North Branch, and a few other small communities where farmers gathered to visit and pick up supplies. We got brief and lasting pictures of the people and towns. An insurance salesman wearing plaid pants and a pink tie beckoned us into his office to give us some tips on getting through the local area. He shared with us a picture of his hog (motorcycle) while his secretary peeked out the window to see if we had really ridden in on bicycles.

We walked into Ethyl's Coffee Shop and sat for a bit to enjoy our morning donut snack and watch the people. Sleepy residents sitting in booths checked us up and down. We overheard two aging, hard-of-hearing buddies arguing about which one of them should go across the street to pick up a pack of Dentyne gum, one shouting to the other, "Keeps your breath fresh!" We wondered why the post office was decorated with flower bouquets—someone had simply wanted to share their late-garden blooms. Later that afternoon a young woman offered us water and a nap under her tree. She said we deserved it for riding all that way. As we pedaled out of town a man in a truck sporting a Canadian flag waved us over. He was lost and asked us for directions. We pulled out our marked-up map and set him on his way, hopefully the right way.

Once again, we were searching for a comfortable spot to sleep. The park in Brown City was home to the Brown City Bloopers baseball team. When we asked at the City Hall for permission, the mayor and police chief conferred for a few minutes and determined no one would mind if we stayed just the one day. We sought out the only sheltered spot with protection from wind, laid out our tent and sleeping bags on the brick floor, and slept like babes in the ball club's plywood dugout.

International Border Crossing. Across the whole continent, political borders had little impact on our travels. Rolling along on bikes we experienced each mile in a uniquely intimate way. The landforms evolved naturally as rivers flowed into coastlines and mountains unfolded as valleys and plains—one continuous changing surface that challenged us, delighted us, and taught us how to conform to the ups and downs and curves and twists even as we ourselves evolved and grew. Getting to know these United States was indeed a fascinating, enlightening adventure.

However, when we reached the Canadian border after riding almost 100 days, we were more than a little taken aback by the reception we received. It took us 15 minutes to walk across the Blue Water Bridge from Huron, Michigan, to Sarnia, Province of Ontario, because bicycling was prohibited. On the Canadian side we walked into the immigration office where we needed to show our driver's licenses. The man asked whether we had ever had trouble with the police. I didn't have a ready answer—that question flooded my mind with memories of being a teen in the 1960s; how many times I was pulled over when I was 18 because I looked too young to be driving a car; the civil rights riots and peaceful protests that I had barely experienced; and the countless times Paul and I had asked for assistance at police stations on this trip. Mixed emotions turned to nervousness thinking about the sheer expanse of country we had traversed, and I *giggled*. Not the appropriate response, apparently, because he sent us over to the Customs kiosk to have our belongings checked.

A stern-looking officer in uniform and overcoat with big brass buttons took our IDs and set to rummaging through my front pack and all of Paul's clothes. He opened film cans, food containers, equipment cases, spreading our belongings out across the wet pavement. The mood was too formal for us, and we were both a little off balance. *How could these people be so suspicious, what kind of assumptions were they making?*

Hadn't we just hung out with the mayor in Brown City, chatting about the Bloopers Baseball Club? What led them to believe we were carrying contraband, drugs, or weapons over the border? Eventually he waved us on, leaving us to repack everything into the panniers and giving a poor first impression of Canada.

Next we dealt with the unfriendly young woman at the Visitor Information Booth who would not speak to us, answered our questions by writing upside down on the map, and shoving brochures through the window slot: no bike riding on expressways, no camping except in official camping areas, and no information at all about trucks or safe bicycle traveling. As soon as we were past the flurry and hassle of the border authorities, we found a park and tried to settle down to have some lunch. The sun that had warmed us in Michigan that morning disappeared behind chilly Canadian clouds as a cold wind picked up. We were on the defensive, and I began to feel a little homesick. Paul chimed in and said we'd be getting to his parents' place soon. Soon enough wouldn't be too soon.

Unexpected Hospitality. Happily, after a couple of hours of riding we arrived at Maitland's Trailer Camp where the friendly proprietor greeted us with a smile. He set us up in a nice, comfortable campsite under a willow tree and gave us a price break on camping: 75 cents apiece. He let us change some of our traveler's checks into Canadian money, which was decorated with pictures of Queen Elizabeth. When the sun rose the next morning we felt better. We'd had a good night's sleep and got off to a better start.

Canada presented us with new sights and practices that I didn't expect. The French and British influence was evident everywhere. American-owned chain stores were familiar. Restaurants served potato chips flavored with garlic and pickles, and a bottle of vinegar was automatically set at every table. Towns were named after places in England, yet the architecture looked a lot like Minnesota. Children spoke perfect English but with French accents. I was surprised to see tobacco plantations for the first time in Canada.

People were friendly when we finally slowed down and opened up. Early in the morning a vacationing camper came to our table and invited us to join him for hot coffee inside his trailer. September brought with it the chill of winter, especially in the mornings. Families out on Sunday drives smiled and waved, seemingly pleased to see us traveling by bike. We were able to find a laundromat in one small town along the way so we stopped to wash and dry clothes during a nice break in the day's ride.

Traffic, including a lot of big trucks, crowded the most direct route through Canada to New York so we were forced to share the road with lots of travelers. But we kept at it and cycled through the entire province in four days. We did notice brownstone two-storied homes with upstairs porches and gingerbread decorating the roof lines. Front yard flower gardens were well tended, and on Sunday we passed many front yards displaying tables and carts covered with fruits and vegetables for sale. We were tempted and stopped at one castle-like mansion where the woman filled our arms with more peaches and plums than we could carry. She refused to let us pay and sent us on our way with a big, enthusiastic wave for luck.

New York State. The day finally arrived when we approached the New York State border. Niagara Falls was just a few hours' ride ahead and we sped out of the Canadian province, excited to get back to the good old U.S.A. We skirted through city blocks lined with tourist attractions, hotels and restaurants, bars, a wax museum, and services for everyone passing by on their way to the falls. Right up to the cliffs of the riverside, neon signs and colorful mural-sized advertisements vied for attention.

Turning a sharp corner, we were suddenly facing a thundering, spraying wall of water pouring down into the gorge. It was breathtaking, beautiful, and at the same time hard to transition from the conglomeration of city businesses to grasp the grandeur of the river. I immediately longed for the solitude of the Rockies and of Yellowstone so I could fully appreciate the wonder of Niagara Falls. We continued on the bikes right up and over the Rainbow Bridge where the U.S. Customs agent waved us through with a big friendly smile from the United States and—we were in New York. We ducked into a restaurant to get out of the cold and traffic and gobbled down hamburgers and sodas. Congratulations and a toast were in order for getting all the way from California to New York under our own steam. Standing at the railing, Paul grabbed a few pictures while I took in views of the immense Niagara River roaring as it poured over the falls—a drop of more than 150 feet.

Journal Entry ~ September 18, 1974 This is Day #100 of our journey. Things have been getting a little tense and we're getting on each other's nerves. I'm always cold and complaining while Paul seems to be always needing to stop and eat. Seems like one of us is always griping about something. We've been sharing how we feel about arriving in New York and have come to the conclusion that we both wish the end of the ride wasn't so close. Paul's thoughts are constantly racing ahead to Montrose, to his family, and a long rest. But he says his thoughts are making him anxious and he isn't sleeping or relaxing when we stop. I, too, am anxious at being so close—knowing that we still have at least a week to go no matter how fast we pedal. Somehow the challenge ahead reminds me of the beginning when we were fighting headwinds in California and looking forward to all the fun ahead. Now, in contrast, we're weary and fighting the chilly weather, looking forward to the comforts of home at the end.

In the midst of so much crazy traffic, we were trying ridiculously hard to stay off the New York State Thruway. Navigating the noise and rush of so many drivers, we might as well have been driving a car. Two nights in a row in New York we stayed in motels because we were just too tired of fighting bad weather and sleeping in the cold. There was definitely an advantage to spending nights in a heated room instead of putting up with condensation collecting on the inside of the nylon tent and listening to wind howling and blowing through the mesh. For our last week, we wanted to be comfortable.

We followed the truck route outside Buffalo, turning east on Route 5 so we would avoid riding through Buffalo proper. We checked in to ask about a better route when we saw the State Police building, and all they had to say was, "Be sure you stay off the thruways." And "Why ride bicycles into New York City, anyway?" We got the usual looks of amazement when we explained how far we had come from California. Skies were darker because of the cloud cover, even when it wasn't raining. We rode past row-houses looking all the same, trees were bare gray branches, and as the evenings came earlier I began to feel a longing whenever I saw the warm glow of lights shining through windows as dinner hour approached.

At a little village called Holcomb, we learned from a roadside placard that the road we were on, Route 20, followed an ancient pathway: "worn so deep by the feet of the Iroquois that it became your road of travel." It had been widened to make it passable for a yoke of oxen, then became a toll road, and eventually was taken over by the state highway system. However this road came to be, it was getting us closer to our goal. The weather and heavy traffic kept driving us to stay in motels, though, and our daily mileage dropped to 40 miles if we really pushed it. We stopped in Ithaca and the Finger Lakes area. The young woman in the motel talked with us for a few minutes about our travels, and then she offered that if Paul registered as a single guest we could save some money on the room rate.

Journal Entry ~ September 20, 1974 *Getting close to the end of the ride, we are acutely aware that in a few days our lifestyle will change completely. Evenings in motels give us more chances to talk about how we'd been getting through these cold, wet, unpleasant days, tired of riding in traffic and focusing on the end in sight. We're both missing the joy of sharing all that beautiful, open country. We agreed that we do in fact have a lot in common, we've learned so much about getting along under some extraordinary situations. Appreciating the beauty of nature always reinforces for us the positive experience of discovery and exploration.*

Riding out of Ithaca on a Saturday, the rain hit just as we headed up a long hill. What began as a mist got steadily heavier the higher we climbed. We were in an industrial area crowded with factories—not a tree in sight. The street was paved in old bricks and we hadn't gotten too far when I rode over a half-inch shard of glass. My tire flattened out immediately so we could not continue. We walked to a nearby community hall and fixed my third flat of the trip under their porch overhang. Then hoping against hope that the rain would let up, we pushed onward to the level top of the hill. Rain did not cooperate. Eventually we gave in and pulled off the road to stand under the eaves of a deserted building where someone had painted a big banner that read "PEACE ☮ LOVE." We considered whether we wanted to catch a ride. In the midst of all the wet and discomfort, I tried to convince myself, and Paul, that it wouldn't be that important whether we pedaled or hitched the last hundred miles.

An Offer We Couldn't Refuse. The next day proved to be a miserable ride to Binghamton. We thought we'd take Route 17 until we could figure out a reasonable alternative to riding in the rain. Another biker, carrying a 22-pound backpack, caught up with us and we rode together for a while. He was from New Jersey, making a 300-mile trip to Syracuse and back. This was his first long distance ride and he told us he'd been sleeping in garages or church basements to stay out of the rain. After about 20 miles we stopped along the highway to talk further before he turned off to continue on his way. As Paul and I stood there after he left, still hoping to avoid another horrible afternoon soaked and cold, a guy in a van-type truck loaded with gallon pots of hemlock trees pulled up. We asked? He offered? Somehow he agreed to give us the ride we desperately needed.

His black tie clashed oddly with the fishing cap, jeans, and checkered short-sleeved shirt he wore. Our new friend, Ben Palto, climbed out of the truck and helped us load the bikes alongside the young hemlocks destined to be planted in his backyard in New Jersey. Paul reminisced about the baby redwood farm we had toured way back in Northern California. We rode with Ben for over an hour and asked about his life in New England. He expressed his frustration, stuck in a rut working as a coffee distributor commuting in the rat race of the city. We admitted to him (and to ourselves) how lucky we were to have the freedom to take this bicycle trip.

He took us to the small village of Monroe, about 20 miles from our final destination. He dropped us by the side of the Bear Mountain Parkway, not too far from the Hudson River. Full of gratitude for the lift, we unloaded the bikes, shook hands, and wished each other luck. It was Sunday, the rain had stopped, and the sun broke through from behind the clouds. We mounted up and easily found our rhythm as we headed down the road that would take us to the end of our journey.

Bear Mountain Parkway. After crossing the Bear Mountain suspension bridge, we rode alongside the steep cliffs and green forested hillsides of Bear Mountain, the closest we would come to the Catskills and the Appalachian Trail. We noticed trees painted shades of orange and bright red—cool nights had splashed the mountainside with autumn color. It was Sunday and watching for traffic added more tension to the day, but the scenery was beautiful and our spirits had lifted.

We had a couple of hours to get to Montrose. Paul's parents lived in an apartment on the grounds of the V.A. Hospital where his dad worked. Along the way we watched for some excuse to stop and gather our thoughts before we arrived. By the side of the road we spotted a funky old white food truck. Painted on the side in red block letters the sign read: "Restore Your Energy at Janie's!" We pulled right up to the side window under a faded awning and ordered hot dogs and sodas. Janie's—the perfect place to restore our energy.

Journal Entry ~ September 22, 1974 At 4:05 this afternoon we walked the bikes into the front door of the Hartman's house. We hadn't called ahead, we just rang the doorbell and said hello to his Mom and Dad. It felt a little tearful, a little joyful. I was crying and laughing at the same time. There was a lot of hugging. We were all quite speechless. Paul and I posed for a picture, wearing cutoffs, standing in front of our loaded-down bikes parked right there in their living room. Written on my face—and shining through Paul's eyes—every inch we pedaled together in pursuit of that mystical horizon, every magical moment we shared will be with us forever.

Afterword

After arriving in Montrose we rested up—literally not moving for a week save an occasional walk around the grounds and along the Hudson. One day we rode the train into New York City together so that I could blindly knock on doors of publishing houses, armed with a big smile and the unlikely tale of being a writer and wanting a book contract about our 4300-mile bicycle trip. I never got past the reception desk of two bonified publishers and totally chickened out at the third address located behind a green wooden door down a dark alley, never even knocked on the door.

Undeterred, we made a plan to spend the winter months with my relatives in Rhode Island where we could figure out our next steps. Paul's mom let us tie our bikes to the top of her sedan and she graciously drove us to Providence—a three-hour drive. We pulled the bikes down, gave her hugs and kisses, and cruised joyfully along 25 miles of the Wampanoag Trail from Providence to my grandmother's house on the banks of a marsh in Warren. My uncle was outside feeding his calico cat, Queenie, when we triumphantly pedaled into the dirt drive. He looked up, said, "Oh, hi," and continued with his chores.

Inside, there were plenty of hugs, kisses, Italian spaghetti and meatballs, and much talking and revelry. Grandma offered us the attic bedroom, my dad's old room, until we found a place to live. My parents flew from California to celebrate my 25th birthday, so we borrowed my Auntie Maria's car and my mom, dad, Paul, and I drove out to Cape Cod so that we could dip our toes in the Atlantic just to say we had traveled from coast to coast. It was a drizzly Rhode Island autumn day, so there was no actual toe-dipping.

A few weeks later my auntie Barbie, landed us a one-room studio in the Newport mansion where millionaire J.P. Morgan once spent his summers. Inside our closet in the rambling Shady Lawn Estate, just down the street from The Breakers and the famous Cliff Walk, I crept up a secret stairway that led to the prettiest square cupola wrapped in ten-foot-tall arched windows that let light in on all four sides. We moved a chair, small table, and a borrowed manual typewriter into the cupola perched right above our room. While Paul worked as an assistant photographer in a Newport photo studio, I typed from my journals and began the manuscript that, 50 years later, has become this book.

Paul's Journal #3

The only few pages that didn't get lost in the shuffle.

Wednesday, September 18, 1974 We could be in Montrose in 7 days at 50 miles a day. By Wed the 25th we'll see how close we come. Went through an area of chemical plants that hasn't been visited by fresh air in 25 years. The change from distinct flowers, trees, lakes, smells, out in the high mountains is just amazing. So extreme that I don't understand it beyond the fact that it was the same me that did it. So much traffic but the shoulders are wide and the traffic is at least aware of our being here so it went okay. Got another $10 motel room because it looked like rain and we didn't feel like worrying about the cold. But the sky gave us a great sunset and all the clouds were gone by 8. Not sure if we can rationalize enough or if we should but it sure feels good not to be fighting windy cold weather and we've got enough money so we may hit the motels more often than all the trip so far. Talked to a NY State Trooper who told us next to nothing about the roads but was really amazed at what we'd done so far. We had more "guts" than him, he said. To us, we just did it a day at a stretch, but to him we can only make a capsule out of all 3800 miles and all 100 days and it must really seem amazing.

Thursday, September 19, 1974 Beautiful sunny cool morning good for riding. In Avon for lunch in the shade of their Civil War memorial, with a good view all the way back to Batavia. We seem to have hills or wind neither very definite just that we'd like to make about 200 miles a day and these get in our way. Our great shoulder has gone off into the boonies but traffic is light so no problems, few trucks. Traffic circles and war monuments seem more in evidence. And long tree-lined streets back in the old neighborhoods. Heavy old oak trees that go on for quite a ways. And neat church steeples with bells that sound the time. Got to Canandaigua and had an offer from the police to a free spot in the park. But between the openness of it and all the water rats and mosquitoes we decided on another motel. After half an hour and five miles riding around we found one run by a couple of very nice older folks. He was politely interested in our trip and his wife wished us good night. Haven't had that before. She looks like Grandma Hartman.

Friday, September 20, 1974 Rain this morning, we're waiting a half hour to let it blow by. Not the best by any means for traveling, it's already 10:15. Made it 1 mile to a diner for coffee, it rained once more while we were inside but then let up almost for the rest of the day. Not hard riding on a good road all the way to Ithaca, 60+ miles. Distant rolling country on both sides, Seneca and Lake Canandaigua. Farms never out of sight. It started raining at the bottom of a 2.5 mile hill into Ithaca and we found a motel before we got soaked.

Saturday, September 21, 1974 It drizzled all the way into Richford, we saw some great country following streams and views from tops of hills. Distant fog hanging in valleys is beautiful. We were soaked in Richford so we stuck out our thumbs and got a ride to Whitney Point with one very talkative farmer. Stayed in a classic hotel with toilet down the hall. Later in the evening our talkative farmer came back just to say hi and stayed for an hour. The room smelled like Nana's house with steam heat and fresh linen. Slept like a top.

September 22, 1974 Our ride left us off 20 miles from Montrose, and we pedaled down rt 6 with some 4 million motorists till the Bear Mtn Bridge and the Hudson River by 3:00. The very last river and so much excitement it's hard not to explode. Saw the hospital from up the river and were at Mom and Dad's house at 4:05. 106 days 6 hours from Santa Barbara. Good! Good! Good!! Supper and sleep within 4 walls I can't believe we're here...that is the understatement of the last 106 days.

Friday, September 27, 1974 Went out for our first bike ride since arriving. 2.5 miles down the road for a spaghetti lunch. Bikes were next to naked and felt awkward but the wind in the face and good strong legs made us both a little homesick for a frame of existence that temporarily stopped as we rolled into this trip's destination last Sunday. Now family and friends will be close around and we'll need much of what we learned on the trip to keep us pushing along for 50 to 70 miles a day along the way toward our first published book. My dad asked what I thought was the favorite spot on the trip. I explained that by virtue of having done the entire trip on a bicycle, everything—every event, every place, every person—was directly a part of the whole. Idaho was very much a part of Oregon was a part of Wyoming. So close and intimate as to be inseparable. There can be no high point of our trip because there really was no single event on the way across.

A good ride.

We saw much.

And learned beautiful things.

Not exactly different, just not the same person.

A trip like this can be the beginning of a whole new way, it shall be for Lynn and me.

October 5, 1974 Bike trips, like 4000-mile ones, are addictive. Some things we find here are just padding and unnecessary. Bike riding kept us living every day to its fullest. Fighting against some of those 4000 miles makes the living deeper.

Acknowledgements

This dream that I've had for more than half a century has become a reality at last, thanks to a lot of people who offered me their encouragement, wisdom, and time. I don't know quite how to thank everyone for your gifts because so much of the work I put into this story came from the invaluable help and support of others.

Thanks to my two brothers Dave & T. Joseph, because you were right there with us the day we took off from Santa Barbara with all the confidence that we'd make it to the East Coast. We did it, thanks to the love and support you two and Mom and Dad sent us—every day of the trip—and every day since. David, thanks for taking a dive into the ocean first, when you wrote and published your book, "Loaded Barrels," and then challenging me to write mine.

A big thank you to Barbara Shovers for opening the door and lighting the way for me to begin the process of memoir writing before I realized I was ready. You have a wonderful way of seeing the best in a person and encouraging creativity. This book might well have waited another ten years if not for you.

To the few people willing to read my developing manuscript, I owe a special thank you for your helpful suggestions as you reviewed the rough drafts. Chris Carmichael, you are the only other bicyclist to read and review my chapters. You kept me honest in recreating the memories that occasionally coincided with your own touring experience, and for that I'm grateful. Mary BeachamHall, a fellow explorer in the world of self-publishing, I thank you for your insights over the years, always with a kind word and positive encouragement.

Kristen Grund Jokinen, I cannot adequately express how much you and Ville have been my inspiration since the day I met you on your book tour, when I read "Joy Ride," and began following your global biking odyssey. Thank you for being the adventurers you are, and for reading through the almost-final version of my book. Keep on biking!

A huge thank-you goes to my Memoir Writers Critique Circle friends: Carrie Hargrave, Jamie Nielsen, Barbara Williams, and Laura Jones. You opened your group and your hearts to me. While writing together, offering support and constructive criticism, we've formed a special bond. Thank you for your time and your valuable suggestions, and most especially for your encouraging words.

I am lucky to have a talented designer in the family. My daughter-in-law, Nina Parsons Hartman, created a perfectly spoked bike wheel for me to embellish all the chapter headings. Sierra, thanks for your keen eye and advice on the images we've included.

To all of my family: Brandywine, Neyah, Sierra, Nina, and Paul, and to my three bright and shining grandchildren—all fellow explorers in this life—I am so thankful I have you. You brighten my every day.

Author's Note

My original journals and early manuscripts served to jog my memories as I wrote this account 50 years after we made the journey. All the stories recounted here are true, but the names of people we met have been changed. Paul took nearly a thousand photographs and we chose the best ones to produce a slide show at the end of our trip which we shared in Rhode Island and in California. We worked together to choose a few photos to include in this book. You can find lots more at our website:

https://www.lynn-natal-hartman.com/